Sacred
SPACES

★ ★ ★

*My journey to the heart of
military marriage*

★ ★ ★

CORIE WEATHERS

D1378237

Elva Resa ∗ Saint Paul

Cover photo of Matt and Corie Weathers ©2015 Kristin Espinosa.
Cover photo of Boeing C-17A Globemaster III 09-9212 operated by
US Air Force ©2015 Corie Weathers.
Back cover selfie ©2015 Corie Weathers.
Back cover map image @2016 Landsat, map data @2016 Google.

All Bible verse quotes are from *The Holy Bible, New International
Version*® (NIV). Copyright © 1973, 1978, 1984 by Biblica. All rights
reserved.

Editors: Terri Barnes and Marly Cornell
Designers: Andermax Studios and Connie DeFlorin

The views contained in this book are those of the author only
and do not necessarily represent the views of the Chaplain Corps,
the US Army, the Department of Defense, or the United States.

Library of Congress Cataloging-in-Publication Data

Names: Weathers, Corie, 1977- author.
Title: Sacred spaces : my journey to the heart of military marriage /
    Corie Weathers.
Description: St Paul : Elva Resa, 2016.
Identifiers: LCCN 2016021699 (print) | LCCN 2016028310 (ebook) |
    ISBN 9781934617335 (pbk) | ISBN 9781934617342 (epub ebook) |
    ISBN 9781934617359 (kindle ebook)
Subjects: LCSH: Weathers, Corie, 1977- | Army spouses--United
    States--Biography. | United States. Army--Military life. | Soldiers--
    Family relationships--United States. | Afghan War, 2001---Social
    aspects.
Classification: LCC U766 .W38 2016 (print) | LCC U766 (ebook) |
    DDC 958.104/74092 [B] --dc23
LC record available at https://lccn.loc.gov/2016021699

Printed in United States of America.
10 9 8 7 6 5 4 3 2

Elva Resa Publishing
8362 Tamarack Vlg., Ste. 119-106, St. Paul, MN 55125
www.ElvaResa.com
www.MilitaryFamilyBooks.com

To Matt:
May this book be the beginning of
actions above words, grace in imperfection,
and new sacred spaces we share together.

To our boys:
May our story reveal to you
just how hard we fought for our family
while serving others.

PROLOGUE

What began with an invitation to go on a one-week trip to learn more about deployment became a journey that changed my perspective of my military marriage.

In the fall of 2015, US Secretary of Defense Ashton Carter was preparing for a holiday tour to visit troops serving overseas. Realizing that military families have more questions than answers about the deployment experience, Secretary Carter's staff wanted to invite a military spouse to go along on this trip to observe, record, and share the experience. Johnny Michael, who was in charge of communications and engagement planning for the secretary of defense, reached out to Kate Dolack, editor-in-chief of *Military Spouse* magazine, to find a good candidate. Kate offered my name. Earlier that year, I was named the 2015 Armed Forces Insurance Military Spouse of the Year, an award given by *Military Spouse* magazine for my professional counseling work with military marriages.

In November when I received the invitation to accompany Secretary Carter, Matt and I and our two young sons were preparing for our second move within six months. Although the logistics would be challenging, we agreed I should accept the opportunity. I was honored to be considered and began developing strategies to use the journey to learn more about deployment and better understand its effects on military couples like us.

Before Matt and I were married in 1999, I asked his mother, who had then been married more than twenty-five years, how I would know if I loved Matt enough. My parents had divorced when I was young. Although I was sure Matt was the one for me, I wondered if I knew what it took to sustain a loving, successful relationship for a lifetime. Matt's mom told me the kind of love I wanted was not the love I could have right then.

"The love you want," she said, "doesn't happen until you have made it through some of the worst of what life has to offer. It comes after years of taking care of each other through ups and downs, after raising children together and tending to them when they are sick. It comes after getting jobs and losing jobs, taking care of aging parents, and overcoming the struggles you have as a couple. The love you have now is just the beginning, and perhaps it is enough to begin."

I have carried those words with me, though I didn't recognize their prophetic wisdom until they played out in my own marriage. Matt and I have seen our fair share of ups and downs. We've obtained jobs and lost jobs, started our family, moved multiple times, gained friends and lost friends. My husband's career as an Army chaplain, which began nine years into our marriage, added another dimension of joys and challenges. But when Matt and I walked down the aisle, we could not have anticipated the stress and impact that deployments and separations would have on our relationship. We didn't know what challenges life would hand us or how to navigate the resentment and hurt—the frequent by-products of conflict. This commitment was not for the faint of heart.

After his first deployment, my husband came home changed. I was different, too—altered by my own experiences while we were apart. Coming back together after a year of unshared experiences was incredibly challenging. After the second deployment, we learned to navigate around these unshared experiences as if we led double lives—our together life and our intermittently separate lives. Learning to love each other through the challenging times, as my mother-in-law suggested, was harder than we expected.

When a service member is deployed, families at home can only try to imagine the life, surroundings, and experiences of their loved one. Service members may describe as much as they can about where they are: the terrain, the bathrooms, meals, living conditions, sights, smells, and people they meet. Even with such descriptions, family members' impressions are likely to be mistaken or incomplete. Perhaps service members don't know how to describe aspects of their deployment. Some can't share details for security reasons. Spouses and families may not know what questions to ask, or they might be too consumed with managing life at home to ask any questions. For many reasons, families are often left with a limited picture of deployment, possibly never knowing how far it departs from their service member's reality. Military family members at home capture what they can, taking details from their service member, adding images from the news or other sources and putting the pieces together.

I had pictured a particular deployment experience Matt described to me, only to realize later, when he shared the same story in more detail over dinner with friends, that my impressions were completely wrong. Sometimes I heard him tell stories to others that he'd never shared with me—like the time he said the local monkeys were cute, until they attacked soldiers. I had no idea soldiers came in contact with monkeys in Afghanistan.

Once, Matt mentioned he had a turkey-and-egg-white omelet every morning. I'd wrongly assumed he had nothing but powdered eggs for breakfast for a year. I pictured him in a room with walls similar to the walls in our home until I saw a TV documentary showing soldiers surrounded by plywood partitions riddled with bullet holes.

Images matter. Details matter.

In my work as a licensed professional counselor with military couples, as well as in my own marriage, I've noted that misunderstanding increases when less sensory information is communicated, particularly during deployment. For Matt and me, video calls provided more productive communication than emails or regular phone calls alone.

Memories are stored in the sensory parts of the brain. Deep inside the brain, the hippocampus collects specific memories through the five senses—sight, hearing, taste, touch, and smell—putting them together to form a single episode, a solidified pattern or connection that forms that memory.

The amygdala, a small almond-shaped collection of neurons nestled right up against the hippocampus, plays a role in processing emotions. These two work closely together to create and preserve memories, connecting emotions with the sensory information. Memories that are strong, whether positive or negative, are often connected with sensory information. An odor or sound connected to a particular memory brings back the memory with startling reality.

When I was a new military spouse, our brigade chaplain invited me along with other members of our family readiness group to the field where our soldiers were doing what I like to call a deployment dress rehearsal. The experience brought several military acronyms to life. We were able to walk into the tactical operations center (TOC), watch the computer monitors, drink bad coffee, warm ourselves at the space heaters, and eat meals ready to eat (MREs) in a makeshift dining facility (DFAC).

We watched the soldiers enact a combat simulation resembling a game of laser tag. When a soldier was "wounded," medics performed their duties as if they were in an actual casualty situation. That one-day experience provided a dimension of understanding that stayed with me during the deployment that followed. When Matt said he was eating MREs at the DFAC, I could picture the setting. When my husband said he would be spending the day in the TOC, I pictured him safe, warm, and well-informed, because I had spent time in a TOC, albeit in a training situation. I could picture the action, hear the noise, and smell the stale coffee.

Now, thanks to the Office of the Secretary of Defense, I was offered an opportunity to see actual deployment locations. With my TOC experience in mind, I wanted to make this trip a multi-sensory experience, both for myself and for any spouses who followed my journey. For this project, my strategy was to report about what I saw, felt, smelled, and touched each day during my trip. I would use those details to share my experience with families and spouses at home, as well as to increase my own connection to my husband's experiences.

Military spouses like me, who are not service members, rarely have a firsthand glimpse into the active duty world. We might see office life while our active duty spouses are home, ruck marches on post, and perhaps listen to gunfire at the firing ranges. But deployment is where my husband's military training and his spiritual fitness are put to the test. At some point over the years, I realized I could not understand every part of his career and ministry because there would be so many moments I couldn't share.

Military spouses often miss large chunks of life with our service members, that may include intense, life-changing experiences. During deployment, military members can be gone for months at a time, sometimes in extreme environments. Traumatic events can shape each spouse in different ways. Each may experience major milestones or setbacks in personal growth. When the service member returns home from a long absence, he or she may be on a different path, physically, emotionally, spiritually, psychologically, and even socially, from his or her spouse. These unshared experiences have consequences. Behind confidential doors, spouses were telling me distance was growing between them and their service members, and resentment was filling the void.

Although a week-long trip as part of the press entourage for the secretary of defense differs vastly from deployment, many of the feelings my husband and I experienced before, during, and after this trip mimicked deployment. For the first time, I would be able to experience in a small way what my soldier felt, and he would see life on the home front with new eyes. I planned to record a raw video journal each night with my reflections of the day to post on YouTube. I would use the audio to add to my Lifegiver Military Spouse Podcast, write a blog for my personal website, and use Twitter and Facebook in conjunction with *Military Spouse* magazine's social media, to report on my trip in real time. I wanted to hit as many platforms as possible. After my return, I would write a cover story for the magazine about my trip and what I learned.

Any trip for the Office of the Secretary of Defense involves a high level of strategy, national policies, and world politics. Secretary Carter undertook the journey, in part, to thank deployed troops for their service. Along the way, he would also engage key coalition partners in the world's battle against terrorists known as the Islamic State. The members of the press with whom I traveled covered these topics thoroughly. My role was not to cover policy or politics; I was there to be eyes and ears for other military couples, to tell the stories I hoped would make a difference for all of us.

As much as I was going on this trip as a correspondent for military families, I deeply wanted this experience to have a positive impact on my own marriage. Matt's exposure to combat losses and death had changed him, and a portion of his innocence and heart were sacrificed in Afghanistan.

I am proud of my husband's service to our country and his excellence at his job. I am also proud to be a military spouse, but I was not happy with the consequences of war in our marriage. I resented the territory it took up between us, the spaces that were sacred to us individually, because we experienced them separately. I was unhappy about the ways deployment changed us and our relationship.

Also, I had grown weary of the demands of military life, the constant unknowns, stressful surprises, and continual change. For years, I had been pushing down my needs to make room for the needs of my soldier. It seemed the military was always telling me it was not my turn—not when my soldier was gone, and I had the stressful job of holding down the home front; and not when he returned, and I needed to cushion his transition to life at home. In the cycle of deployment and training, absence and homecoming, it seemed my turn would never come.

As I packed my bags and prepared for this journey, I knew that if I wanted to see my marriage differently, I'd have to leave behind my resentment. If I wanted to help other couples develop healthy relationships, I had to pay attention to my own. I needed to trust what my mother-in-law told me was true, that mature, lasting love is forged not by avoiding hardships, but by sharing the struggle side-by-side with my husband. My mission was to take back the lost ground between Matt and me, ground we had surrendered to hurt, misunderstanding, loss— and to Afghanistan. Ultimately, this is the mission of every marriage: The pursuit of understanding a spouse's wounded heart, the humility of forgiveness, and the journey from pain to restoration.

HEEDING THE CALL

The packers were coming in a few days. I'd been cleaning out drawers and rooms for two weeks while my husband was at work and our two sons, ages eight and eleven, were at school. To say I was tired was an understatement. I was about to snap.

Our family was in the midst of a convergence of major events. Christmas was three weeks away. We were about to move to a home we had never seen. Adding to the upheaval, I had accepted the invitation to travel with the secretary of defense to visit military members and families in Turkey as well as deployed troops in Iraq and Afghanistan. Officially, I would be part of the press corps, documenting my journey for *Military Spouse* magazine. I looked forward to sharing what I would learn with as many military spouses as possible, to help them better understand their own service members. But unofficially, I would be on a journey to connect with my husband's deployment experiences.

My time and energy was focused on the move and preparations for my trip. I tried to calm my growing anxiety by running, eating sensibly, and taking supplements to communicate to my adrenal gland that I still wished to be friends.

I was frustrated that Matthew and the boys were not giving their best efforts to help me complete my pre-move checklist. My repeated requests for our sons to perform simple tasks to help went unheard. Instead, they spent their time wrestling, knocking things over, and giggling endlessly. I knew that some of this behavior was the result of their own nervousness about moving, once again leaving behind a place that was familiar and comfortable. Our time at Fort Jackson, South Carolina, had been short, only five months. Even so, the boys made good friends to whom they had grown attached.

I planned to be home when the movers came to pack our household goods, but I'd be gone when the shipment arrived at our new home in Virginia. My husband would handle the delivery and the kids' first week of transition on his own. I knew his stint as keeper of the home fires would be brief but intense. I had handled these same tasks many times before. But this time, the roles were reversed. I was leaving, and he was staying.

I didn't actually doubt Matt's ability to handle everything. I was stressed because I didn't have the control I was used to having over the details of our move. I wouldn't be there to ensure the furniture, rugs, and dishes were placed where I wanted them when the movers showed up at our new home. I wouldn't be able to give my full attention to our boys' emotions during their transition. I wanted to keep all the plates spinning my way.

I wanted my pre-move checklist complete before I left for Iraq and Afghanistan. I had already finished Christmas shopping and wrapped the presents, hoping that after I returned we could ease into the holidays. But I was already second-guessing what I bought and whether it was enough. The preparations for the trip were time-consuming and worrisome. Due to the tight operational security on a trip for the secretary of defense, I couldn't have access to the schedule or the specific locations I would be visiting. I didn't know what to wear or how to pack.

Although I had become accustomed to handling uncertainty as a military spouse, I was feeling the weight of a different set of unknowns. I was on the edge of what I thought could be a major life-changing opportunity, and I felt a weight of responsibility. I hoped I was prepared. I feared I was cracking under the pressure.

My husband stopped me as I was removing pictures from the living room wall to sort and pack. He said, "I think we need to sit and talk."

I took a deep breath and sat on the couch. I was irritated at the interruption. What I really needed was for everyone to move faster to match the pace I'd set for myself.

Looking at me as if he knew something I didn't, Matt said, "This is all part of the process. I know you feel bad for leaving, but I will be fine."

I was shocked. He was reading me all wrong. I didn't feel guilty about leaving on this trip. I was just anxious about getting everything ready for the packers.

At least, that's what I thought.

"These last-minute tasks that you are stressing about are not worth it," Matt continued. "You are leaving in two weeks, Corie. Think about it. You may know that you are going to be safe, but the only thing the kids know is that another parent is going to Afghanistan. We need to cut them a break. The priority at this moment doesn't need to be the house."

He was right. The last week had been tiring for all of us. I had expected the boys to help, but I could see I was demanding too much from them.

"If you are going to experience what it is like for a soldier," Matt continued with a knowing grin, "then take note: *this is all part of the process.*"

He had said it again: *part of the process.* What did he mean by that? *What process?*

Up until this point, I had been focused on seizing this opportunity—even at what seemed to be an inopportune time—working out the logistics and strategy on short notice. I had planned for clothing, visas, a passport. At a military supply store, we bought boots, a jacket, and pants suitable for visiting Iraq and Afghanistan. My strategy for the trip was big picture, thinking about how this trip could impact other spouses. I hadn't had a chance to process my own pre-departure feelings.

As I looked into my husband's eyes that evening, emotion flooded me. I hadn't really thought about what this trip meant for Matt, for me, and for our boys.

Although my week-long absence couldn't compare to the magnitude of a full-length deployment, the days of preparation and stress were very similar for our children. I had conflicting emotions about leaving my family during a difficult time. I thought back to the days just before Matt left for his first deployment. It happened to be the week of our oldest son's birthday. Crappy timing, but we didn't have a choice.

Allowing myself to sit in the pocket of my thoughts, I realized I was feeling guilty for leaving Matt alone to receive our household goods. Anyone who has been through it knows how stressful it can be for one person alone to direct boxes and furniture to the appropriate places, to watch for damaged boxes and missing pieces, to be sure items are reassembled correctly.

Though my dad agreed to come up and help out with the move in, that didn't decrease my feeling that I was abandoning my husband at a critical time. I knew Matt would work himself to the bone trying to take care of all the boxes before my return. I knew I couldn't stop him, because he would do exactly what I would do if he were the one leaving.

I have usually been the parent who quickly senses when one of the boys is not doing well during a transition, and I wasn't going to be there. I'd miss the initial excitement and sadness as they entered their fifth new home. I wouldn't be there to accompany them on their first day at a new school, to see them say their shy hellos to their teachers.

At the same time, I felt the excitement of leaving on a new adventure. I believed my decision to go on this trip was the right one. I knew my skills were a good fit for the task at hand. I was excited about what I would learn and how I'd use what I discovered to help military spouses in their own marriages.

I wanted to go.

I wanted to stay.

I wanted to get on the plane, because I was called to do it, to show my children that fulfilling a calling means making difficult choices.

I wanted to run from the whole thing and choose family, just to prove to them they were the most important thing in my life.

I wondered if this was what Matt experienced before each deployment. I thought about the difficult push and pull he must have felt before he said goodbye to us for a year. My heart filled with a new understanding. I felt gratitude for his willingness to do a job he loved, even though it pulled him away from us. I more clearly understood how his love for us must have ripped out his heart when his departure was imminent.

I had always assumed it was difficult for him. But now I was beginning to understand why he seemed to pull away from us in the days before he deployed. He was readying himself for the pain of leaving while anticipating the fulfillment of a mission he was called to do. Only a calling that meant a great deal to him would take him with such excitement toward the mission and away from us. I felt a similar push and pull.

On one of our first dates when we were in college, Matt took me to a tiny Italian restaurant close to campus. He asked me what I saw myself doing in the future. I told him that growing up in our church, I had encountered a particular couple who worked together, traveling around and encouraging marriages. They inspired me by their ability to work together. Because of my own family history, I longed to invest in marriages. When he heard that, Matt sat back in his chair and looked at me. We grew up less than 150 miles from each other and, although we didn't meet until college, Matt had been inspired by the same couple! He also dreamed of helping couples strengthen their marriages. We knew it wasn't a coincidence. This was evidence of the bond forming between us.

In an ironic turn years later, the couple who had inspired both of us divorced. Their relationship crumbled after years of putting their ministry before their own marriage. This news only furthered our resolve to have a strong marriage. We wanted to be sure we didn't follow in those footsteps.

Matt and I spent the early years of our marriage in Lexington, Kentucky, taking turns working and putting each other through graduate school. I studied for my master's degree in counseling. Matt planned to go to seminary to study Greek and Hebrew to pursue a career in academia, but early in his studies he began to question that career choice. Teaching Greek and Hebrew no longer felt like the right fit. He loved studying the Bible and loved serving people, yet he didn't feel called to be a teacher or pastor.

One day, Matt came home from the gym excited and said he'd met a former Special Forces soldier who was studying to go back into the Army as a chaplain. For the first time, Matt knew what he wanted to do. He felt a call to become a military chaplain. When he told me about it, I did not share his enthusiasm. Joining the military represented a major change in our plans. Matt would need to finish seminary and complete a period of practical ministry experience to become a chaplain. He agreed to put his final decision on hold for a year or two.

With a new sense of purpose, Matt continued to pursue the degree he needed to become a chaplain. A year later, with my blessing, he signed up for the US Army Reserve. I hoped that becoming a chaplain in the reserves would answer the questions he had about his calling and ministry. I could tell he needed that answer like he needed air. I had to love him enough to let him go. And I did.

Matt's first step was to attend a fourteen-week basic officer's training course for chaplains at Fort Jackson. As we ate dinner together the evening before he left, I tried to imagine those weeks and months without him. We had never spent so long apart, and I was pregnant with our first child. When we talked on the phone while he was away, I heard the sound of fulfillment in his voice. After he came home, he never doubted his calling again.

I needed a little more time.

One Sunday, the pastor of our church preached a sermon that ended with an unusual statement to the congregation: "If you aren't called to stay, then go."

Matt and I had never heard a pastor tell people to leave a church. Those words cut through both of us like a knife. We were happy in this church, but we didn't feel *called* to *stay*. We had an opportunity to serve in a church in Atlanta near my family, where Matt could fulfill the pastoral ministry requirement he needed to become a chaplain. We took a leap of faith. With hardly a dime, we packed up the car and our toddler son and moved to Atlanta.

Over time, Matt became even more convinced that the Army was where God wanted him to serve. While Matt worked at the church, I worked in my first local private practice, completing requirements for my licensure. Everything around us should have made us more satisfied, but something still wasn't right. I knew my husband felt called to the military, but I was not yet convinced. I reluctantly went with him to a dinner for chaplain recruits. Matt was preparing to turn in his final paperwork to request a slot as a chaplain.

At dinner that night, I had an overwhelming feeling of peace in spite of my previous reservations. I felt like we belonged to something, or at least as if this was where I wanted us to belong. At the end of the evening, I pulled Matt aside and said, "Okay, let's do it. But if we do, we jump in with both feet and go active duty."

Of course, he wholeheartedly agreed. He had just been waiting for me to catch up.

Matt turned in his papers in June 2008. He was soon accepted for active duty and given a choice of two units. One was in Alaska and included a deployment immediately after our arrival. The other was in Colorado and gave us nine months to become settled before Matt left for his first deployment. We chose the Colorado assignment to allow a little more time to acclimate to a new home and military life before the deployment.

In August, we arrived at Fort Carson, so excited to be a military family serving military families. Matt was assigned to 3rd Squadron, 61st Cavalry Regiment, one of six battalions within the 4th Brigade Combat Team (4BCT) of 4th Infantry Division (4ID). We had no idea how choosing 3-61CAV would affect the trajectory of our lives.

All these years later, I was hearing my own call to "Go." I didn't have military orders, but I knew I needed to heed the call. For years, in my office as a licensed counselor and in my life as a fellow military spouse, I had supported and counseled military spouses on whom multiple deployments had taken a toll. I thought about that toll as I recalled the phone calls from Matt during his first deployment. I remembered how I strained to understand the details of his life over there. The distance between us grew every time he talked about something I couldn't feel, picture, or experience. After a while, I was less tuned in during those conversations, and I gave Matt less than my full attention. I accepted the gaps between us as part of the military experience. We were living separate lives, and we had separate memories.

Separate memories caused problems when he returned home. Even casual conversations had hidden pitfalls. We found ourselves comparing whose deployment experience was more difficult or significant. Our arguments were more about each wanting to be heard by the other. Finally, we resolved to simply respect our separate memories.

Surviving some moments during Matt's absence took every bit of courage, grit, and independence I could muster. There were moments during that first deployment in which I could not have survived emotionally without intervention from a friend or loved one. Matt had no way to understand my experience. He had placed his friends' remains in body bags, and there was definitely no way I could understand *that*. We desperately needed the other to understand. Yet we hit a wall when we tried.

We began to call these times "sacred spaces." This gave us terminology and neutral territory to say to each other, "I've been through something so big that I'm different because of it. I can't change that, but I need you to tread lightly when I talk about it. You can't fix it, and we definitely can't ignore it." We are all changed by experiences, particularly those we cannot resolve. We live differently because of them.

I learned to ask questions when he "zoned out," usually a signal that he was reliving or processing difficult memories. Whether he opened up or not, I tried to be protective of him through the rest of his day. Likewise, he learned to accept that my sacred spaces were just as significant to me, though my memories of challenges at home were far different from those he faced in Afghanistan. Spouses at home can also experience life-changing moments, sacred spaces, without threat of gunfire.

"Sacred" comes from the Latin word *sacrare*, meaning "set apart, revered, regarded with great respect and reverence." We acknowledged that one experience could never compete with another, and we resolved to respect those sacred spaces even when we could not fully understand them. We handled these spaces carefully because of the emotional gravitas surrounding them.

Sacred spaces surround moments that can be both positive and negative. I have talked with service members who vividly recall a battle they survived and someone else did not. I know of people who felt they would not make it through a battle, but they felt God's presence stronger than at any other moment of their lives.

During deployment, I remember military spouse friends of mine who huddled together during a frightening time, knowing there had been an incident, waiting for the knock at the door, not knowing whose soldier had been injured or killed. A strong part of that memory is the love and community of support, not just the fear. Other memories that become sacred are as simple as a sunrise, or as life-changing as the birth of a child. Relationships are strengthened by shared experience, especially significant ones. Deployment, by its very nature, creates highly significant yet separate experiences for military couples.

After Matt came home, we were surprised by how many sacred moments we had each collected while apart. Respecting and navigating around these sacred spaces in our lives seemed like the best thing we could do. Recognizing the presence of sacred spaces matured us over time and improved our communication. We processed what we could learn from them.

We began using the phrase, "Everything is grist for the mill."

Grist is corn that is taken to a mill to be ground into flour. Every part of each kernel becomes part of the final product. In the same way, no matter what we went through individually or together, no matter how difficult, we chose to look for the purpose from the experiences.

My experiences while Matt was deployed gave me confidence. I learned that I could do what I had to on my own. Because of his experiences, Matt embraced the fullness of life and became more sentimental. I thought this made us better, stronger people.

Using what I learned to help others, I tried to validate the experiences of other military spouses, and Matt did the same for service members. Eventually, though, I began to wonder about the cumulative effect of subsequent deployments and separations. Could having so many sacred spaces bring harm to military marriages? Could anything be done to close the gaps forming between us, and between other spouses in their marriages?

The gaps in my marriage had amplified the call I was hearing. For myself and for other spouses like me, I wanted to learn what I didn't know, to see what I had never seen. I wanted to know what changes a trip like this could make in my relationship with my husband.

I wanted to go.

I wanted to stay.

By choosing to go to Afghanistan, I was choosing to pursue a better understanding of my husband. I could not say no. I wanted to heed the call.

I looked into my husband's eyes, a man who had been in this place before.

"It's all part of the process," he said again.

A day or two before the packers were due to arrive, I was dusting the house, not only because it was long overdue, but also because it eased my anxiety. The stresses of the past several years, the moves and deployments, had worn us down. We had attempted professional counseling at a previous assignment. Although it was helpful, we were never in one place long enough to make progress. We had hoped Matt's five months at school—without deployments or training—would give us time to regroup and rest, but it didn't happen. We were a family in need of respite.

With my mind on these anxieties, I dusted carelessly, barely noticing what I was doing until a crash brought me back in the moment. I took a step back, looked down, and gasped. A small ceramic plate had fallen from its display stand on the living room table, shattering into pieces. The plate, adorned with an angel sitting on a globe carrying a banner reading, "On Wings of Gratitude," had been a gift from a Gold Star widow.

I sat down on the floor and stared at the shards for a long time. My thoughts were sucked through the black hole of my tunnel vision, focused on the broken object. *How had I been so careless? Why didn't I have it in a safer place?* Tears blurred my vision as I began picking up the pieces, trying to recover every shard. To others, it was just a plate. But to me, it symbolized a sacred space in my life, a moment of emotional gravitas. This plate was a reminder of the time I spent with a new widow in her darkest moments, a sacred place set apart from the other moments of normal life. I sat with her when her life was shattered. Not every situation can be fixed, and hers could not. I couldn't bring her soldier back. I couldn't put the pieces back together, but I could sit with her there in the mess.

I put the pieces of the shattered plate on the kitchen counter and waited for Matt to come home.

When he walked through the door, he saw the pieces on the counter.

"I didn't know what to do with it," I said. "I can't bear to throw it away."

"No," he agreed firmly. "We are going to glue this back together, because that's what we do. It's who we are. We take the shattered pieces of people's lives and find a way to mend them."

He was right. *That* was our calling, a calling that came from our own unexpected brokenness. Our mission included sitting in the painful moments of other people's lives—to be able to say to someone, "You are not alone."

We each knew what it was like to have our hearts drop to the floor, experiencing something so painful, so life shattering, that we weren't sure how to put ourselves back together. Some experiences just don't make sense, but we decided if we didn't have reasons for those experiences, we could instead draw purpose from it. Grist for the mill. Everything is usable. Out of great pain and suffering, gratitude and hope can still claw its way to the surface.

Whenever Matt and I found our strength running dry, we held up four fingers and said "Fourth Quarter." The gesture started out meaning, "Push through! It's almost the end of the game!"

But as time went on, it became a signal of resignation to a game that would never end. We went from hoisting four fingers up high with a "Come on baby! Fourth Quarter!" to sluggishly lifting four fingers and saying nothing at all.

For some time, I'd been telling spouses it was okay to not understand, okay to respect sacred spaces from a distance. But I no longer wanted to believe the gaps could never be closed. I wanted a better answer. I was ready to stop avoiding the space between my husband and me. I needed to sit in the messiness of whatever was ahead of me.

RIPPING OFF THE BAND-AID

Military couples know the contrasting emotions during the days before a deployment—and the agonizing tension. We dread the moment of separation, yet long for the moment to be over, for the goodbyes to be done. While we want to enjoy every second remaining before departure, at some point it's better to rip off the Band-Aid. I would only be away from my family for one week, longer than I had been away from them in quite a while, but a far cry from the length of Matt's deployments. I'd experience various theaters of military operations in relative safety, again much different from my soldier's combat zone experiences. My mission, to walk in Matt's shoes to at least have a glimpse of deployment from his point of view, included getting ready to say goodbye.

I tried to pay attention to my feelings and those of my family as I prepared for the trip so I could compare them to past conversations Matt and I had before his deployments.

Five days before my "deployment," I was still distracted. We were living in a hotel room on Fort Jackson. The plan was to drive to Virginia right after Matt's graduation from his career course. Along with what we packed to last us until the truck met up with us at our new home, I had to pack separately for my trip. I had packed and repacked everything several times in my anxiety over forgetting anything essential or packing something in the wrong place.

I was thankful for Matt's experience living out of a duffle bag and his expertise at cramming a large volume into a small space. I had four pairs of shoes because I didn't know yet where I was going, and I had received a message about potential business casual events. I briefly envied Matt's deployment packing, where boots were the only option. My mind was racing between having everything ready, attending to the kids' emotions, trying to be excited for my husband's graduation from the career course, and welcoming Matt's parents who were coming for the event. There was just no way to be fully present for everyone the whole time.

Thinking back to Matt's predeployment days, I wondered if he was really good at compartmentalizing his own emotions. Perhaps he decided to think about it later on the plane. Or perhaps he took more time to process it.

He took me outside to the hotel parking lot and told me that while I was gone he wanted me to keep my eyes forward on the mission and not worry about my family at home. He said, "I am not going to write long emails about everything that is happening here, because I want you to focus all of your energy on what you need to do first."

"But I want to know how you are!" I pushed back.

"I know," he said, "but I know how much it will require from you. I want you to know I am releasing you to it."

I realized then that he was making it his mission to experience my side as a spouse. Time froze for a moment as I allowed myself to feel the weightlessness of his permission. I knew it did not imply that in a real deployment the service member should not need to hear from the family. It was more about having permission to look forward and not second-guessing by looking back. Heeding the call may look like momentarily taking our eyes off those we love, only to return fully knowing what is most important in life.

I suddenly felt selfish and guilty that so much of our life of late was about me. Everything, it seemed, revolved around "the trip."

I did my best the next day to be present for Matt on his graduation day. I had been so busy I had forgotten to get him a graduation gift. I raced to the store that morning for the materials to make him something. I ended up presenting him a crappy homemade Christmas ornament to mark our time at Fort Jackson. Despite my effort at trying to make it about him for a change, his graduation day was sabotaged by a botched alteration to the tactical pants I'd bought for the trip. We were supposed to begin our drive to Virginia immediately after a celebratory lunch with Matt's parents, so I had to get the problem fixed.

While they began lunch, I attempted to convince military alterations to replace the two new pairs of pants I needed. Panicky and in tears, I got back just in time for the meal to be served. Matt put his hand on my knee under the table to calm my body from the alterations altercation, and I fell in love with him all over again.

As we started our drive to Virginia, I was multitasking on the phone with the magazine people regarding last-minute strategy, and then with the defense secretary's office, finally receiving the itinerary of the locations we would visit. Matt drove in the other car with the boys so I could have quiet for the calls. His grace, patience, and servant heart continued to amaze me. *Had I done anything like this for him before his last deployment? Had I been this patient and forgiving?*

Unknowingly, I started over-compensating by apologizing and trying to smooth out anticipated issues before they were even real. The constant apologizing for the inconvenience of it all was not helping us. The situation was all too familiar.

I thought about Matt's permission in the hotel parking lot. Having permission from loved ones makes a difference. *Had I given Matt permission to focus on his mission?* Knowing our family would be fine at home released me from the worry that I was abandoning them. Even though we were apart, we would get through it together. Matt had given me permission. Now I had to give myself permission to fulfill my calling.

Later that evening, I shared the schedule and locations with Matt. One of the stops was Jalalabad. I knew the name; he had referenced it many times during his deployment and over the years since then, usually calling it simply "J-bad."

"Jalalabad?" he exclaimed. "You are going where we were!"

He was excited, but I wasn't sure what it meant. I knew he had primarily been at Forward Operating Base (FOB) Bostick. During that deployment, our brigade commander's wife had made 4ID 4th Brigade t-shirts for the spouses. Matt suggested enthusiastically that I take my shirt with me. He showed me pictures of J-bad, pointing out a memorial he said was at the entrance. He thought it would be great to have someone take a picture of me with the memorial. I tried to share his enthusiasm, afraid to tell him I didn't know where J-bad fit into the story of his deployment to Bostick. Acknowledging that would only emphasize I missed an important detail. My anxiety increased as I realized how little I knew about where I was going.

Military couples know that conflict before a deployment is all but guaranteed, often culminating in a blow-up argument. I wondered if this would happen to us as the day of my departure approached. Perhaps my expectation of an argument triggered it, but there were too many other stresses going on for it to not happen.

We spent our first night in Virginia in a hotel. We woke up that morning to cool crisp December air, sunny skies, and mountains in the distance. We were ready to see our new house and start our new adventure. Matt and I held hands and sipped coffee as we looked out the windows into the woods.

"I can see us loving it here," I said.

It had been a long time since we'd had a happy and stress-free moment, and my first mistake was thinking it would last. My "It's a new day" mentality only lasted until Matt and I walked back into the hotel room we shared with both boys.

Children act out their stress in all kinds of ways, usually the one least expected. During this transition, our boys did not stop talking. Every thought in their heads came out of their mouths. Matt and I could not have an uninterrupted conversation when the boys were awake. The four of us were crammed together in one hotel room, which made private time nearly impossible. Matt strategized ways for us to steal a moment or two. I knew he needed me close as much as the kids did, but he allowed everyone else's needs to come first.

We all got in the car to go see our new house, and everyone's differing plans for the day began to collide. The tension level rose. Our peaceful facade slipped away. I compensated for Matt's grumpiness with annoyingly positive chirpiness about everything.

"What's going on, Hon? What do you need right now?" I asked in a whisper, adjusting the car stereo to play music in the backseat for the boys.

"It doesn't matter what I need," he said. "It's not about me right now. I'm trying to make sure three other people have what they need."

Grace and patience were wearing thin. I wanted us to have a peaceful, happy day together, but instead we were sitting on a ticking time bomb, waiting to see who would finally set it off. The only reason we didn't lose it was because we had no place to argue in private. Besides, experience had taught us a thing or two about what was really going on with each of us. I wanted a blissful day with him, and he just wanted me. The stress of packing and driving was over, but our time and space were filled with two kids who couldn't stop talking.

Throughout the day, I reflected on how we had switched places. I kept trying to make sure every family member was happy, each getting his own share of my attention, only to be frustrated when it didn't work. I knew what Matt was about to walk into for the next week while I was gone: more incessant talking, the chaos of receiving household goods on his own, and very little contact with me. I also knew how hard he would work to make the house perfect for me.

I was trying to serve him and give him as much rest as possible before I left, he was trying to do the same thing for me, and neither of us was willing to receive. I appreciated that Matt was trying to "release me to the mission." He was taking my calling to go on this journey as seriously as I was.

Shame came over me. I regretted I had not treated him as thoughtfully before his deployment departures. I regretted not pushing down my own needs and serving him more selflessly. I wanted to step back into those days and listen to him ramble about his fears, concerns, and plans, and sit with him as he packed and re-packed.

I honestly don't remember what I did or didn't do back then, but I know I was filled with uncertainty before he left, probably clingy and focused on my own needs. We knew more now, and we could make better decisions going forward, but we couldn't change the past. Matt knew what he had needed before deployment, and he was now providing it for me. I needed to let go of trying to please everyone and receive what he was doing for me.

There is no one right way to prepare for a goodbye, because

it is not separate from the other stressors of life. Departure doesn't wait for perfect timing in a family's life. It just shows up. When it does, everyone has needs, all of them important. Perhaps the best thing we can do is not ignore or suppress our own needs, but to be aware of each other's needs and take turns giving and receiving love.

The next morning, Matt and I ate breakfast in the hotel restaurant while the boys watched television in the room. During our brief chance to reconnect I told him how much I wanted him to take care of himself and how much I wanted him to let me take care of him, too. He thanked me again and spoke affirming words of love for me and confirmation of the importance of my trip. He wanted me to know what it was like to move forward, while feeling the guilt of leaving family behind. The best thing he did for me when he deployed was trust me to hold down the home front. I aimed to do that for him by trusting him to make household decisions while I was gone. I chose not to try to control him from a distance.

He gave me over to my mission, and I trusted him with the mission at home. I told myself I would give this opportunity everything I had while I was away, prepared to be fully present, and then available to Matt again when I got home. The lessons I learned about pre-departure stress would guide me the next time Matt had to say goodbye.

The departure point for my trip was Joint Base Andrews, Maryland, within driving distance of our new home. My departure was scheduled for a Sunday, the day before our household goods would be delivered. But then I was informed that the secretary's schedule had changed. Departure was delayed twenty-four hours. I was leaving the same day our household shipment was due to arrive.

To fill the extra day before us, Matt suggested we explore the Natural History Museum in DC. As we perused the exhibits, I pulled him aside to thank him for planning something to distract us. Before his departure for deployment, we often had to sit around and wait for his time to go.

"Are you nervous?" he asked, hugging me from behind and kissing my neck.

"Yes," I admitted sheepishly.

"I'll let you be small today," he said, "but only for today. To-morrow, you have to be big again."

Several times throughout the day, Jack, our youngest, asked, "How are you, Mom?" It was his way of checking in. I told him each time that I was good, and I was glad I would only be gone a week. He held my hand most of the day and asked me a thousand questions. Our older son, Aidan, crowded out the worries bouncing around in his brain by reading, sometimes out loud, every placard on every exhibit in the museum. He did the same with nearly every street sign we passed. Back at the hotel at JB Andrews, where I would stay the night, the boys were still talking nonstop. Five miles of walking around DC hadn't diminished their nervous energy. We all needed to rip off the Band-Aid and put the goodbye behind us.

After they prayed over me, it was time to go. I watched them walk to the car from my hotel window. I imagined the release Matt would feel driving away. I knew that relief, we both did, when the waiting and the tension is over.

I tried to push away every horrific thought of anything that could go wrong while I was gone, to me or to them. I wondered if I had time to update my will or write letters to Matt and the boys in case something happened to me. I had been overseas before, but flying on a plane to the other side of the world didn't feel the way it had before I was a mother.

This better be worth it, I thought. I remembered a message Matt wrote soon after he left for his first deployment.

June 22, 2009, 8:09 a.m.—Afghanistan

> *Today was the first day that I really thought about missing hugs from them. I can't really say that I have allowed myself to get sad, I just try and stay busy and productive. I really want this year to count, so my motto for every day and every meal is to make it count.*
>
> *~Matt*

I took a deep breath and reminded myself of my mission. I walked away from the window and whispered my commitment: "Make it count."

DEPARTURE

I woke up at seven o'clock Monday morning without an alarm. Show time at the Andrews passenger terminal was 1:30 p.m. Again I had too much time on my hands. I watched the news, drank my coffee, and went for a run to work off my nervous energy and recon the terminal where I would go later that day. I washed laundry, packed, and repacked my bags a few times.

I had thought carefully about what to bring. I had a suitcase with my clothes and Matt's small camouflage rucksack to hold items I wanted to keep with me at all times. He had taken this rucksack everywhere with him for trainings and deployments and had a nametape sewn on it that said "WEATHERS." There was something sweet about taking the backpack Matt took to Afghanistan on this trip. It made me feel like he was with me. Matt had attached a Wonder Woman keychain to one of the zipper pulls. He said it was his way of sending me as his Wonder Woman.

Inside the backpack, along with my laptop, phone, and iPad, I carried a stuffed animal our oldest son received when he was a toddler, Brave the frog. Brave is purple with yellow on his belly and the soles of his feet. On one foot, embroidered in purple thread is his name, Brave. Aidan held him close on doctor's visits or any other time courage was required of a little boy.

Shortly after Matt left for his first deployment, the boys and I were struggling to find things to send him in a care package. I asked Aidan, then five, what we could send. He proudly nominated Brave. We decided Daddy might benefit from some of Brave's courage, so we stuffed the frog in the box and sent him to the other side of the world. We hoped Matt would send a few pictures of Brave's adventures in Afghanistan, and he did not disappoint. Brave visited the mortarmen in the mountains and traveled in Matt's backpack on many visits to other troops. We received one picture of Brave passed out on his cot after a long day of traveling. Later, Matt sent Brave back home again. It bridged the distance between us to know we could send Brave, see him there with Daddy, and then have him sent home.

Brave was showing some wear from his years of love and his travels around the world. The boys brought him to me a few days before we packed up our house and suggested I might need him during my trip. This morning, I was especially glad to have him. I hoped that new adventures for Brave would add an element of fun for my kids back at home and for the troops I hoped to meet.

Also in Matt's backpack, I carried one of my grandfather's handkerchiefs. My grandfather was the patriarch of my family and a father figure to me. Our time together was always filled with deep conversations and truthful talks about life and faith. Deep in my memory, I carried a picture of the embroidered "R" on the handkerchief ever present in his suit pocket at Sunday morning church. When he died, I asked for his handkerchiefs. For the past three years I'd kept one in my purse. In this small way, when my tears welled up, he was still there to comfort me. Knowing that my trip would sometimes be emotional, Matt reminded me to bring along one of my grandfather's handkerchiefs.

One of my grandfather's stories about me was about a time he offered to help me, but I responded with, "I can do it myself, Granddad!" I remember Granddad telling this story to Matt, and then letting out his giant laugh as if it was a part of my character he was proud of. Holding on to his handkerchief was a reminder of his belief that I could do big things.

The trip's schedule said we'd take off from Joint Base Andrews and head straight for Turkey. Since the flight would be more than fourteen hours, plus time in Turkey, I packed another change of clothes in the backpack and my new hiking boots. This was going to be a long day, more like two days rolled into one. My loaded backpack was heavy, perhaps too heavy, but I wanted to be prepared.

Eventually, it was time to meet up with the secretary's staff and other journalists at the passenger terminal. When I found the meeting place for the rest of the entourage, Major James Brindle, a spokesman for the Department of Defense, and Johnny Michael greeted me with smiles. The room had leather chairs, sofas, a large-screen TV tuned to CNN, plus coffee and snacks. While we waited for the rest of the press to arrive, Johnny explained the dynamics of the group, which would include the US Secretary of Defense Ashton Carter, the secretary's wife Stephanie, members of the secretary's staff, a cadre of journalists representing various news outlets, and one military spouse—me.

He said they had not before had a military spouse on one of these trips who was not part of the secretary's staff and not officially press. Because I was writing content for *Military Spouse* magazine and for my own platforms, I would be considered part of the press group. Johnny said they also planned to find ways for me to experience what I needed to fulfill my mission, which was to see the deployment environment and relate my impressions to other military spouses. This part, he explained, would have to be handled carefully to avoid the appearance I was given privileges the rest of the press corps did not receive.

The journalists would report on Secretary Carter's duties on the trip, and the secretary's staff would serve as liaisons between the defense secretary and the press as well as plan and carry out his meetings with leaders of the military and various countries. I was to report on my own experience rather than the secretary's. I hoped to also have opportunities to talk to some of the service members along the way.

As I sipped on coffee from a styrofoam cup marked with the Great Seal of the United States of America, journalists began to funnel into the room. Each found a seat, opened a laptop, and immediately began working. The only way I could have introduced myself would have been to interrupt their work, which looked pretty important. More members of the secretary's staff arrived as well, and although they had mentioned wearing khakis and jeans for the plane, all were dressed in business attire. I was thankful the journalists were dressed casually.

As the journalists pounded busily on their keyboards, I

watched television. CNN was broadcasting President Barack Obama's remarks following his meeting that morning with national security advisers at the Pentagon.

Referring to thousands of airstrikes conducted by the US and coalition partners against Islamic State terrorists, the president said the military was "hitting them harder than ever." Attacks on civilians in Paris and in California in the previous weeks had placed military efforts against the terror organization in the forefront of the news. The president mentioned the nations helping in the fight and stressed the need for more support from others in that region.

"And that's why I've asked Secretary Carter to go to the Middle East—he'll depart right after this press briefing—to work with our coalition partners on securing more military contributions to this fight," said the president.

On the television, Secretary Carter stood just behind the president. I realized I had a front-row seat for a potentially historic moment.

I thought back to Matt's deployments. How strange that I could live like nothing was happening in the world beyond the stress going on in our little home and family, while another member of our family was making a difference, playing a part in significant events on the other side of the world. I wondered if Matt had a sense, when he was flying across the ocean, that he was joining something much larger than himself.

I opened my laptop and tried to look as busy as everyone around me, but I had nothing to work on yet. I had prepared social media blurbs about my trip, as had *Military Spouse* magazine, but we had to wait for the okay from Johnny before any of the news could be released. Johnny drafted a post for us ahead of time that conformed to the operational security (OPSEC) requirements of the Office of the Secretary of Defense.

Matt texted to ask if we were still going to J-bad. I asked Johnny and he said probably not because of the shift in our schedule. From Matt's response, I knew he was disappointed.

When it came time to ride the bus from the terminal to where we would board the plane, Johnny gave me the okay to spread the word. Hurriedly, I texted my family to tell them how much I loved them and texted the magazine that we were a "go" to announce my departure. Blasting out all the texts and prewritten social media blurbs distracted me for a few minutes. Afterward, the frightening thought of something tragic happening during this trip flashed again through my mind. Again I wondered if I had enough time to scramble a note to my kids about how amazing they were and how I believed they could still change the world even if something happened to me. Fortunately, I managed to regain my self-control and professionalism until I stood on the tarmac and looked up at the giant Boeing 747 E-4B with "UNITED STATES OF AMERICA" emblazoned across it.

I believe my words were, "Holy shit, this is happening."

Climbing into this beast was like going back in time. The aircrew in their flight suits and the smell of the plane reminded me of my dad, a retired Air Force Reserve pilot. It took me back to my childhood, when I tried on Dad's flight mask and breathed in the musty odors of the rubber mask and the jet fuel that infused all his gear.

I boarded on one set of service stairs alongside members of the press. Another staircase, complete with red carpet, was reserved for the secretary of defense, his wife, and closest advisers. Air Force pilots and crew in their flight suits surrounded the stairs on one side of the plane.

Inside the plane, a narrow hallway ran down the right side. The main part of the plane was divided into rooms. I assumed the front section was for VIPs. The second section was set up like a conference room. The third had seating for the press. In this area, three rows of seats faced forward. I found one in the back row with my name tag on it. Three seats in front of the room faced three computer stations, which looked like throwbacks to the 1980s. I later learned that these stations were originally used to monitor nuclear threats from the air.

The fourth section was partitioned off, but had windows allowing me to see the cubicles, computers, and monitors inside. This room was reserved for the secretary's staff, who were very friendly and checked on me every so often. To my relief, some had changed into more casual attire, so I felt less underdressed.

We all took our seats and prepared for takeoff. On the front wall of the press section, two giant TVs broadcast ESPN and

CNN until we were over the ocean and out of range. The outside world was only visible from one airplane window, and I wasn't near enough to see out of it. I had no reference to show me how high or fast we were flying. That was probably a good thing.

Within the hour, Secretary Carter emerged to make a statement to the press regarding the day's events and the president's remarks. A journalist on my row asked if she could have the aisle seat so she could record what the secretary said.

The secretary greeted me with a smile and shook my hand to welcome me on the trip. He cracked a few jokes with some of the journalists who had probably covered him before. I stood to listen while he made his official statement. The journalists held out microphones, cameras, and tape recorders to capture his words.

Secretary Carter spoke with a sincerity I appreciated, reviewing his purposes for the trip. He said he would speak with battlefield commanders to get their assessment of the situation and meet with his counterparts in other nations to strengthen partnerships to combat terrorism. Our first stop would be Incirlik Air Base, Turkey, a hub of operations in the US Central Command Region due to its proximity to Syria and known strongholds of Islamic State terrorists.

While reporters put their equipment away and I returned to my seat, I thought about the strategic chess match between world leaders and the part that would be played by military members and their families.

Our schedule for the day in Turkey included a town hall meeting, where Secretary Carter would meet with families stationed at Incirlik. Because of potential terrorist threats in the region, military families were confined to the protection of the air base. The town hall format provided the secretary with an opportunity to gauge how military families were coping in that environment, as well as allowing families to ask questions and be heard.

The press had the option of attending the town hall, which was off the record, or meeting with American and coalition pilots on the record. All of the journalists chose the pilots. I chose the military families. I wanted to be there with them, to listen even if I could not report what I heard.

At the outset of the fourteen-hour flight from Andrews to Incirlik, a piece of paper was passed around for each of us to write identifying information and what size armor plate we needed, a sobering reminder of the potential hazards of our journey.

The journalist in the aisle seat next to me fell asleep early on, but I couldn't rest. I was too excited. I watched the plane's course on the TV screens in front. The E-4B received an air refueling during the flight, but the one window didn't allow a view of that. Though excited, I was not nervous. I felt secure in the presence of an entire crew of Air Force service members.

We were served an early dinner. Around midnight Eastern Standard Time, breakfast helped us begin the transition to new time zones. After the first day's stop in Turkey (Eastern European Time), our home base for the week-long trip would be a hotel in Bahrain (Arabia Standard Time). We would return there each night for a few hours of sleep between subsequent flights to Iraq, Afghanistan, and the Persian Gulf.

After breakfast, I debated whether to sleep for the remaining five hours of the flight. A staff member encouraged us to try and rest, but I didn't succeed.

FAMILY BONDS

After a smooth landing, courtesy of the US Air Force, I stepped into the bright sunshine of 10:00 a.m. in Turkey. My body, still on Virginia time, thought it was 3:00 a.m.

At Incirlik, more military planes than I could imagine were on display on the tarmac for the secretary of defense: C-130s, F-16s, F-15s, A-10s. Fighters were being loaded with an array of armament, preparing for more of the airstrikes the president mentioned. I said a silent prayer for the pilots and took note of my surroundings. I was close to the front lines, and the enemy was not too far away.

The noise of the fighter jets taking off rumbled in my chest. I couldn't help but feel thankful for what they do and the amount of skill and precision of the pilots. Families are exposed mostly to their own branch of service so, as an Army spouse, I'd rarely seen the incredible power of our military aircraft firsthand.

The journalists departed for their interview with the pilots. I followed the group bound for Secretary Carter's town hall meeting at the base's new community center, where approximately 100 military family members had been waiting for some time to hear more about the lockdown they were living under. Like many military families stationed overseas, they had come to Turkey alongside their service members probably hoping to enjoy local culture and perhaps travel to other parts of Europe and Asia. Instead, they were unable to leave the confines of their military installation. Months earlier, all the families at Incirlik had been given the option to return to the States, though their active duty members had to remain. Many families left. As I spoke with a few of the spouses who had chosen to stay, one told me the lockdown had been going on for more than 100 days, and the families wondered about a possible mandatory evacuation of military families.

Military families stationed overseas often say the best part of the experience is the close-knit nature of the military community abroad. Families I met at Incirlik told me their current situation created a crucible, bonding them together to support one another. Incirlik was a wonderful place for their children to play and grow, they said, embodying a true village mentality.

I thought about the new spouses, for whom the good and the bad of this experience was their first taste of military life. Tough times often create the most connective memories. Many of my military spouse friends flashed through my mind: a neighbor whose ten-year-old son shoveled the snow in my driveway without being asked, another neighbor who wrestled with my sons when Matt was deployed and the boys were in need of a little fatherly rough-housing, and spouses who gathered for the holidays when our soldiers were away. The adversities of military life forge forever friendships. Some of the families at Incirlik would look back and value the friends they made while confined to the base more than they would value the grand sights of Europe. They were creating their own sacred spaces, living in uncertain circumstances and relying closely on each other.

I was moved by the fact that these spouses and families were on a mission much more extensive than my one-week foray. This was their home. They lived here with their children, up close and personal with the battle against terrorism. The families shared the stresses and risk and saw the everyday work their spouses did on the front lines. The evidence was as near as the flight line, as loud as the roar of jet engines, as tangible as the odor of a flight suit.

I recalled my visit to the TOC when I was a new Army wife. In a similar way, the spouses here were experiencing with all of their senses the jobs their service members were trained to do. In the spouses I met at Incirlik, I saw the confirmation of my theory that the more information and understanding families have about the mission and the environment, the more supportive they are able to be to their service members. Many of the spouses there described how much better they understood deployments, because at Incirlik they watched a deployment play out in front of them. Crew members on the ground and in the air put in long hours in support of the high tempo of ongoing operations.

Our time at Incirlik was also on a high ops tempo. We zipped from location to location on the base. Like the military families I met there, I was awed to see troops executing actual missions rather than just training.

At lunchtime, we walked through a dining facility with twenty minutes to grab a bite. As I sat down, I stilled my thoughts and deliberately took in the sights in this first dining facility, or DFAC, I'd been in overseas. I barely had the chance to recognize that I was in another country. This particular tent, filled with rectangular tables for about six people each, easily accommodated forty to fifty people. A hand-washing station was at the front, as I would discover was the case at many DFACs, often with a foot-pedal-operated faucet. I thought about Matt's stories of excessively washing his hands to combat germs and sickness during deployment.

At an aircraft hangar later, I rejoined the other journalists. While I was at the town hall and DFAC, taking in the experience of being on foreign soil where families and troops were serving their mission, the reporters had written about the news that impacted their mission and filed their reports for the day, turning in copy and video to their editors.

The Turkish government had only recently lifted its banned use of this air base on Turkish soil for strike operations against the Islamic State. In the hangar, we heard the roar of jets taking off to carry out those airstrikes. This strategic location allows American and coalition forces greater immediacy and efficiency compared to other locations in Europe.

By afternoon in Turkey, I had been up for more than twenty-four hours, give or take a bit of sleep snatched on the plane. It was Tuesday morning in the States. Because I participated in the town hall, I missed an opportunity to have access to Wi-Fi with the press group. I had to wait until we arrived at the hotel in Bahrain that night to contact Matt. This is when I realized what contact with the outside world, including my husband, would be on this journey: sporadic and not up to me. I would connect with my family when I could. It would happen or not happen. I didn't have a way to notify Matt that I had arrived somewhere safely. He just had to trust that all was fine unless he heard otherwise.

I had been in his situation so many times before, waiting for news at home. It was unnerving to be on this end. I didn't want him to worry, but I was powerless to do anything about it. I'm usually the one with my phone attached to my hip, waiting to hear from him. Something told me Matt would completely understand.

By now, my dad would have arrived and our household goods delivered. I hoped everyone slept peacefully for the first night in our new home. I thought about the many times Matt tried to reach me during deployment in the middle of the night on the off chance I would hear him and wake up.

September 16, 2009—Afghanistan

Hey Love,
I don't think your messenger is working on your phone,
I have been trying to contact you for the past thirty minutes.
I am still here if you would like to chat on Skype!
~Matt

Jet noise was a constant throughout the day. The missions didn't stop just because the secretary of defense was in town. Secretary Carter spoke to a large gathering of coalition troops in a hangar near the flight line. At several points, he had to pause until he could be heard again above the deafening, and reassuring, roar. Each time, the airmen smiled proudly at one other. It seems the cool factor doesn't wear off, even for the Air Force.

Another cool factor for me was seeing airmen from other countries joining our airmen in the same cause. Military troops from Germany, Spain, and Turkey were present at the event. At one point, several coalition airmen stood up and thanked our US military for their hospitality, saying how proud they were to be fighting alongside them.

At home, I watched the news when I could, but two-minute segments on the news is hardly enough to understand complicated world events. I had never fully understood the role of coalition partnership in our efforts against the Islamic State.

Seeing countries on the front line working together and serving side by side gave me a sense of the larger integrated mission.

Matt had traveled to Australia to train with their military and later worked with them during his second deployment. I remembered he mentioned meeting members of the Latvian military during his first deployment. Even though I wanted to give myself grace, considering the fact that I had been at home parenting toddlers at the time, I realized I had not taken in that part of his deployment, his connection to other nations as well as to world events.

I sensed that I was watching history unfold, seeing the people and countries that were making it happen, observing moments that might someday be in history books. In school I thought I hated history, but history was alive and fascinating from this perspective.

Tuesday afternoon, we boarded the E-4B for Bahrain. I had been with the Air Force all of the long Monday-blended-in-to-Tuesday. I got a taste of the understandable pride of Air Force families—something incredible to witness. From the moment I stepped on the plane at Andrews, watched the aircrew in action during the flight, then took in the sights and sounds of the flight line at Incirlik, I was moved by their focused attention and excellence.

As I sat back in my seat, thinking about my dad, who had flown in and out of Incirlik as an Air Force pilot, it seemed I had been seeing him all day around every corner in his green flight suit. I love my father deeply. He grew up on a farm in Kansas with dreams of flying planes. He committed himself to reach that dream to soar in the clouds. Dad is a quiet man and lives his life with the values he learned early in the military. He and my mom married young and depended on the Air Force for support as an active duty family. While we were stationed at Charleston Air Force Base, South Carolina, he flew a C-141.

He later left active duty to join the Air Force Reserve, and we moved to Atlanta, Georgia. Dad flew several days a week as a Delta Air Lines pilot and spent one weekend a month flying C-141s out of Charleston AFB. He was gone a lot. Eventually, I learned not to expect him to be home for my birthday or Christmas, so I could be surprised and happy if he was there.

I struggled to understand why he wanted a job that took him away so much. I wondered if he liked flying more than he liked being a dad. I felt deep inside that couldn't be true, but no other reason made sense to me at the time.

When my dad came home, I searched his luggage for peanuts from his Delta trips. I told him one day I would go on trips and bring him peanuts. A few times, my brother Shane and I went with him to Dobbins Air Reserve Base near our home in Atlanta to watched him land the big green C-141 and take off again, carrying other reservists back to Charleston.

I wasn't a true military brat, but I was proud of what my father did, and he was, too. Perhaps I thought flying was only something Dad *had* to do to pay the bills. I remember asking him why he loved flying so much, wondering if he would either affirm my fear that he loved it more than me or admit how much he hated that it pulled him from home. It was an unfortunate trap set up by a child. He never fell for it. His response was usually something about the excitement of flying above the clouds or seeing the earth below. He told me that rainbows really don't have an end, that they are circular. From the ground we can only see an arc, but he had seen them from the sky. I knew he saw the world in ways that few can. My brother wanted to be a pilot just like him, but I didn't understand it.

As I grew older, I felt a disconnect with my father. I wanted him to choose family more. Every now and then, he had an uncomfortable sound in his voice that said he was trying not to become emotional. He'd tell me how sorry he was for missing Christmas or my birthday because of his flight schedule. The situation was obviously painful for him. Maybe he hoped we would one day understand why he loved to fly so much. By the time I became an adult, my father and I had developed a wonderful relationship. I still didn't understand the passion behind what he did, but I knew he loved us and wished he could be in two places at once.

Now surrounded by members of the Air Force, I felt camaraderie as though I belonged with them. I couldn't see a plane take off the runway without thinking of my father and how he would feel if he could be there with me. He would have been full of immense pride and curiosity about the planes lined up on the tarmac. When I talked with the Air Force families about the demanding schedules of their service members, I wished I could call Dad and ask him about some of the missions he flew. I wished I had paid more attention when I was little to the stories he told me, to the sound of excitement in his voice, expressing how he had been a part of history.

As I sat in the plane flying toward Bahrain, Dad was with Matt, helping him with the move. He understood our military lifestyle and was completely supportive. Now retired, he's always there when we need him. Perhaps my marriage wasn't the only relationship that would find healing this week.

Back at the hotel, I wrote a post for my blog, recorded a video about the day's experiences, and posted everything to my webpage. I'm not sure how the journalists met deadlines like this all the time. The video upload would take five hours. I settled into the hotel room and chugged two bottles of water. During our busy day, there had been little time for bathroom breaks, so I had been hesitant to drink much water.

I was able to connect with Matt via Wi-Fi at 9:00 p.m. in Bahrain—1:00 p.m. in Virginia. Matt said he was doing well, unpacking boxes, and putting together some new furniture. After he and the boys left me at Andrews, they had stopped at IKEA to buy some things for the new house. We had chosen some items in advance, but when he sent me a picture of the new rug, I cringed. It was not the gray one I had chosen to accent a favorite painting of mine. He picked out a brown rug because it matched the furniture. I resisted the urge to comment. I needed to let it go.

During one of Matt's deployments, I had to buy a car. I had purchased countless household items while he was away. I'm sure there were moments he disagreed or would have chimed in on a small decision, but he left those decisions to me in order to focus on his own mission. I was thankful for all he was doing to get the house together. I would learn to love that scratchy burlap carpet and give thanks for a thoughtful husband every time I walked on it.

As jet lag set in, I felt sorry for those whose work required frequent travel like this. I was thankful for those who provided food on the plane and encouraged me to eat. It helped me adjust to differing time zones and kept my blood sugar at a healthy level. So many people played a part in the day's success. I was grateful for each one and grateful to be part of the mission.

On the plane we received the itinerary for the next day's events, which would take us to Iraq. I knew I needed to rest in preparation for another long day, but I lay in bed that night, wired and awake. I thought about how our service members are provided the basic necessities they need to keep functioning. Even when they aren't hungry, they are encouraged to eat regular meals, sometimes not knowing when they'll have another opportunity. I'd heard from those who've been there that deployment is rarely convenient. It's filled with "hurry up and wait" moments. The first day of my journey had certainly exemplified that. I was at the mercy of the schedule and the people in charge.

Matt sometimes says that vacations and weekends are important to him, because he gets to make choices for himself throughout the day. If I really imagined what deployment was like for my husband, I could begin to appreciate the little things: a cold bottle of water, a good cup of coffee, a convenient bathroom. I took an Ambien the Pentagon doctor on board the plane had prescribed, another measure to adjust my body's clock. My mind was racing with everything I had learned, and this was only the end of Day One.

VISIONS IN A C-17

I tossed and turned through four hours of sleeplessness in spite of the Ambien. The sound of racing cars in downtown Bahrain didn't help, neither did my anxiety over the YouTube video, which still hadn't uploaded. I had set two alarms on my phone and also asked the hotel to provide a wake-up call. I didn't want to be late and risk being left behind at the hotel. Looking at the day's timeline, I saw that the secretary was meeting with national leaders in Iraq. He would meet with various leaders at each stop throughout the week.

I thought two hours was plenty of time to get ready, but I still felt rushed. My videos were not uploading, leaving me to wonder if I would be able to fulfill my grand intentions and promises to document my experiences on so many media platforms. I decided to leave my laptop in the room, hoping it would finish the upload while I was gone.

Back home in the US, the day was coming to an end. I checked in with Matt as the boys were preparing for bed. He had sent an email about their first day without me even though he said he wouldn't send anything lengthy. I read through it quickly.

December 16, 2015, 2:35 a.m.—Virginia

Good morning Love!

Today went very well! We put up the big tree, Grandpa strung the lights and the boys did most of the ornaments. They have been adjusting quite well. The boys' rooms are mostly done, just need to hang a few things on the walls. Aidan's room looks GREAT! I met some of our neighbors yesterday and today. There was a dad playing hockey with his seemed-to-be four-year-old son behind us. I introduced myself and asked about the basketball goal (whether we are allowed to put it up or not). I didn't find that out, but the dad introduced himself as the P.E. teacher at Jack's new school! We will plan to visit the school Thursday morning on our way to Harrisonburg, where we will hang out before getting in line for Star Wars!

Your dad is doing great, he was a big help putting the boys' shelves together with me today. He did this really cool craft with the boys of putting Christmas-themed cupcake papers on a Christmas light strand and then he hung it up, along with the stockings, under the bar area. It looks really cool.

I am doing well. I know that you are soaking it all in and finding where you can fit in the mix. You are being raised up in consistent and constant prayer.

All my best,
Matthew

I was so glad he sent an update. I was already looking forward to reading it again later in the day. I felt guilty I didn't have time to respond, but I could not be late. Every sentence in that email mattered: the neighbors he was meeting, the way he was organizing, the boys loving their rooms. I was glad they were doing well and so grateful to see the tasks and activities back at home from another perspective. These were the duties that filled my days when Matt was deployed. Now that I was the one who was away, I gained a new appreciation for how important those tasks were. Comforted by the knowledge that Matt was taking care of everything at home, I saw how much those actions and good communication matter to a spouse who is far away. I gained a new appreciation for my own role, knowing that what I did at home made a difference. Those long emails I wrote to him even when I was tired at the end of the day were valuable to him, even if he didn't have time or energy to respond. *Next time he's gone,* I thought, *I will intentionally write more.* But at that moment, I had a job to do. I left my laptop to finish its task, left the "Do Not Disturb" sign on my door for a measure of protection, and went to find breakfast.

I expected to be traveling by helicopter on Day Two and needed to pack light. I decided to carry a smaller backpack with only my phone, tablet, snacks, and lipstick, of course. Once I got in the press van and saw the press still with their laptops, I was wondering if I had made the right decision. My plan was to write and upload social media posts from my phone or tablet when I had Wi-Fi, disregarding the time zone differences. Those following my updates would catch up when they woke up. Pushing out everything all at once at the end of my day was not going to be effective for anyone.

I dressed more casually. After one day, I already knew some of the clothes I brought would not be comfortable or practical, and I wondered what I'd wear for the rest of the week. For this day I decided to wear the tactical pants I had to buy and alter twice. Best investment ever. *These are at risk of becoming the new pants Matt will have to talk me out of wearing every day*, I thought. I also carried a jacket. Now grateful for Matt's insistence that I purchase the correct clothing for this trip, I thought about how much he is a gift to me.

Deployment requires a large amount of gear and clothing—some of which is provided and some of which stretches the budget. Now, even in a limited way, I understood why the right gear makes such a difference. No grumbling from me next time we needed to buy extra equipment or uniforms.

Matt's deployment experiences were filled with culture, people, and food. He shared stories of interacting with locals, children trading him skewers of lamb for bottles of Coke and sharing *naan* bread with the local elders. Our travels in and out of the island nation of Bahrain were my only opportunity to experience the Middle Eastern culture outside a military installation. We stayed in a hotel on the northern tip of the island near the airport. The sights I saw were mostly metropolitan.

When we flew into Bahrain the first night, it was dark. In the morning light, the capital city of Manama was beautiful. Strange and ornately shaped buildings and skyscrapers stood like artwork and countered the sandy beach that lay only across the street from our hotel. I could see the ice-blue waters of the Persian Gulf from my window.

The women I saw in Bahrain mostly wore *abayat*, traditional ankle-length black overgarments. Some wore a *khimar*, an overhead *abaya*, like a veil covering the hair but not the eyes. Others wore a *niqab*, covering all but the eyes. Most of the men I saw were dressed formally in pressed *thobes*, loose,

ankle-length robes made from fine white cotton. The night before, I shared the elevator with a young man of about fifteen
with two younger boys, the littlest maybe two years old, all
wearing beautiful white *thobes* with ornate gold embroidery and
white head garments.

We traveled to and from the airport in a motorcade, usually
at an alarming speed. The homes I could see on those trips represented a range of economic levels, with square white stucco
homes on one side of the street and run-down shacks nearer
the water.

When I found out, even before starting the trip, that we
would fly in a C-17 to Baghdad, Iraq, I anticipated this would be
a difficult part of the trip for me. I struggle with megalaphobia,
a fear of large objects like planes, ships, and hot-air balloons.
The C-17 is a monster of a military plane, large enough to carry
helicopters and tanks in its belly.

When I was a child, I took a ride in a hot-air balloon at a
carnival event. All I remember is looking up into the balloon as
we rose in the air and hearing the very loud blast of the burner.
Since then, being close to large objects has made me want to
run away in terror. My skin crawls to imagine walking under
one. Matt and I had several talks about this leading up to this
trip. Embarrassing myself on this trip was not an option.

On the way to the airport, I knew I had to overcome more
than the fear of the plane. I wanted to be fully present to experience Matt's perspective, and that would be difficult if I were
focused on myself or my fears. This wasn't the first time fear got
in the way of bettering my marriage. Other fears had taunted
me with excuses to not draw closer to my husband: fear of being hurt, rejected, or misunderstood.

The giant C-17 forced me to make a choice. Would I allow
fear to convince me to be a victim or would I choose courage to
experience the joy of connection?

I had been keeping company with fear for far too long. I now
wanted to have experiences I'd missed due to my fear.

When Matt and I lead marriage retreats, we find that fear is
the root issue of a couple's inability to be vulnerable with each
other. Across the board, men and women fear weakness, fail-
ure, rejection, and more. Fear is deceptive. I knew that the C-17

could not actually harm me, but everything in me was reacting as if it could. How many times had I approached my relationship that way, anticipating being hurt? Sometimes if we expect to be hurt, we get exactly what we're looking for.

I was surprised that boarding the E-4B from the ground on the first day didn't faze me. With that small success under my belt, I chose courage and walked right up to the C-17 and marveled as I went inside. Fear was replaced with wonder.

Taking off in the gigantic C-17 was incredible to experience. The inside of the plane was bare-boned compared to passenger planes. Wires and ducts were exposed on the inside walls. The huge interior allows plenty of room for a large volume of cargo, including passengers. For our flight, a large module rather like an Airstream trailer was secured in the middle. The module was a compartment for Secretary and Mrs. Carter and their closest aides. Canvas seats with a bagged breakfast on each lined the sides of the plane. Two porta-potties were in the forward area of the plane, and extra cargo was strapped down behind the module. There were no windows.

The engines made a deafening roar as the plane taxied down the runway. The other passengers and crew wore headphones or earplugs to dampen the noise, but I chose not to. I wanted to take in every sensation. I hoped that allowing my senses to take in the sheer power and sound would register forever in my memory. I was surprised at how quickly the C-17 took off in spite of its size. I would have flown from my seat during take-off if I'd not been strapped in. Whatever maneuvers they made caused my stomach to drop. Everything shook, including the module in front of me. The engines roared as we settled in for the two-hour flight to Baghdad.

Overcoming my fear must have dumped dopamine and adrenaline into my system, because I was ready to celebrate. The crew put out coffee and snacks, and we were able to walk around in the plane throughout the flight. I looked around and realized I was the only one there who didn't have a boss to report to. The journalists around me were already working on their stories for the day. Everyone had a job to do or deadlines to meet. In this blissful moment, the only thing I had to do was simply take it all in and talk or write about it. I was ready to fully embrace the newness of each experience. I smiled and could have skipped through the plane if there had not been so much cargo taking up the gigantic hold.

One of the secretary's staff must have seen the glint in my eye, because he asked if I was having fun. I struggled to find the words to convey how much this opportunity meant to me. This wasn't just taking me along for a ride. This was a gift I could not repay. The staffer appreciated my enthusiasm and took me around the plane, pointing out key elements of a VIP flight like this one. After the brief tour, I sat and talked with a few people and took some selfies. I wanted the secretary's staff to understand how meaningful this experience was to me so that they would feel a confirmation that the decision to invite me was a good one. I wanted them to know that what may be another mundane day at work for them was life changing for me. I knew I couldn't act like a kid in a candy shop all day, but for a moment, I felt liberated.

Back in my seat, I reflected on every detail of the plane, the exposed wires, vents, and the crew sleeping on the floor in the back.

I thought about Matt's role as a chaplain to service members and how the role can often be misunderstood. His job as a chaplain is to provide religious support to the US Army, and to ensure First Amendment rights and the free exercise of religion to the soldiers he serves. Chaplains in all the services advise commanders to ensure these rights are upheld for all service members, including those who do not adhere to any faith. As a Protestant Christian chaplain, Matt conducted chapel services in his own faith during deployment, and he was also there to make sure soldiers of any other religion had the ability to practice their faiths. Chaplains offer counseling and critical stress debriefings after traumatic events, assess the morale of the soldiers, attend to the wounded and dead, and lead memorials for those killed in action. Chaplains live by the tenet, "Nurture the living. Care for the wounded. Honor the fallen." To carry the burdens of so many is a difficult task, and to honor the fallen is especially painful when close friends are among the fallen.

Matt had led ramp ceremonies for his fallen soldiers in a C-17 exactly like this. A ramp ceremony is conducted when the remains of soldiers killed in action are loaded onto the transport for return to US soil. Often the aircraft that carries them is a C-17 or a C-130. Matt had done more ramp ceremonies than he ever thought he would have to. I pictured him in the plane with me, the module in the middle gone and a flag draped casket in its place, and Matt standing near the casket, saying a prayer in a trembling voice. Matt had accompanied the remains of soldiers when they had to be transported by helicopter from a remote location to a base where they could be flown home. I imagined Matt, strapped in his seat aboard a CH-47 Chinook, staring at the container holding the remains of one of his friends.

First Lieutenant Tyler Parten and Matt connected even before the first deployment, sharing a common belief in God and the mission of serving others. Tyler played guitar and was well known for his big smile, energetic personality, broad shoulders, and singing at the top of his voice in the Golden Bee Piano Bar in Colorado Springs after a few beers.

Tyler loved his girlfriend Meg, a beautiful woman with flowing dark hair and a sweet spirit to match. They were in their twenties, with a glow of love and infatuation that was contagious. We shared a table with them at the predeployment ball. That magical evening initiated me into the cavalry world. Meg wore a stunning bronze gown, and Tyler wore a ridiculously large cavalry stetson with his uniform and a huge smile. The ball was a celebration of life and the last chance for everyone to release nervous energy before the deployment.

At the beginning of that first deployment in 2009, Tyler talked with Matt about his relationship with Meg. The deployment was making it difficult for them to stay connected. After talking to Matt, Tyler knew he was ready to propose.

Tyler agreed to play his guitar in the next chapel service at FOB Bostick, since Matt had not found someone to lead worship music yet. Tyler was excited to help, and Matt was eager to accept his help. But on September 10, 2009, Matt called me early, around 5:30 a.m., and said quickly that he couldn't tell me what was going on, but that I would need to be close to Meg and make sure she had everything she needed. He didn't sound like himself, but I was too groggy to connect the dots.

Later that morning, we went into blackout; all communication coming out of theater in that region was shut down. A communications blackout is standard procedure after combat deaths or injuries, giving authorities time to notify affected families appropriately before news leaks out. A blackout is never good news, and spouses at home have no choice but to wait in the silence.

There was a firefight on the mountain during one of Tyler's platoon patrols, and he was shot many times. Due to the ongoing battle with the Taliban, it would be hours before other troops could go in and get him and the others off the mountain. Since Matt's job as a chaplain included checking the bodies of those killed in action, he would be with Tyler.

Matt has talked to me many times about his last moments with Tyler, staring off into the distance as he talks, like he's talking to someone a million miles away. When Matt came home, he said there was a reason the Old Testament says, according to Jewish tradition, a person was considered different after touching a dead body. He felt different. And he was.

Matt still holds images of Tyler's shattered body in his mind and wears a memorial bracelet with Tyler's name on it. It's a sacred space for Matt. Realistic flashbacks of the trauma of seeing his friend that way leave him overwhelmed. He found a kindred spirit in Tyler, who was taken too soon. Matt led a memorial for Tyler so that fellow soldiers could pay their respects and say goodbye. I still can't imagine leading a memorial while managing one's own grief. Matt later conducted a ramp ceremony for Tyler on board a C-17, like the one in which I now traveled.

September 11, 2009—Afghanistan

By far the single most shaping event in my life as a chaplain was memorializing a great friend and brother in Christ, Tyler Edward Parten. The Sunday prior to him arriving in the glorious presence of His Lord, we planned for him to begin leading worship in Chapel, his idea. The relief that I felt to have someone assisting in ministry to the Destroyers of 3-61CAV was eclipsed by the grief felt by our entire community. I cried over him in the belly of the C-17, which would give him his final trip home. After the final respects had been paid to him by all in attendance to the Ramp Ceremony at Bagram, another chaplain nearby put his arm around me as I knelt and repeated the chorus from Revelation Song, *the last song that Tyler praised His Father with before he entered in to praise Him for eternity.*

~Matthew

Years passed before Matt was able to sing even a few words of *Revelation Song.* Tears would take over and transport him back to that time and place. Depending on the day and how close we are to September, he may or may not be able to finish the song. September 10th feels different for us each year, but it's usually a quiet, reflective day.

A few years after the deployment, Matt was asked to officiate Meg's wedding as she married one of her and Tyler's good friends. It was a beautiful way for Matt to bless Meg's life with someone else, as if handing her from Tyler to her new husband. Matt felt he was doing something for both of them by seeing her off into a new chapter. We had planned while we were there to go to Tyler's grave at Arlington National Cemetery. Matt wanted to take off his memorial bracelet and leave it by the white headstone. He seemed to want closure, too. But at the last minute, he decided he wasn't ready. He still wears it today. This first major loss is a daily reminder to Matt to be his best for every soldier he comes across, a reminder that there is great significance in serving this country. People who had plans to love, marry, get a degree, and grow old with the love of their lives died too soon. Matt can't forget. He still has flashbacks of seeing his friend's remains. This sacred space still haunts him.

Sitting inside the roaring C-17, I had a more accurate picture play out in front of me. I could see the draped casket. I could see Matt standing at the tail, ramp down and open to the tarmac. I could see him delivering his remarks, trying not to cry, his chin quivering, knowing he was in charge of such a somber event for his soldiers and command. I could see his sweet face that, at that moment, I couldn't hold. Pain I couldn't kiss away. In my mind's eye, I watched as he huddled over Tyler's casket, another chaplain holding him where I should have been. Where I always thought I would be, but wasn't. I didn't get to hold him for six more months.

A separate memory of Matt on a C-17, sacred in its experience of relief and joy, came during his second deployment. He was invited to come to Washington, DC, to attend the Medal of Honor ceremony for Staff Sergeant Clint Romesha. Clint was being honored at the White House and the Pentagon for his actions in the Battle of Kamdesh, at American Combat Outpost (COP) Keating. He asked Matt, who had been his chaplain, to come and give the invocation at the Pentagon event.

This was a stressful time for Matt for an entirely different set of reasons. He had permission to go, but he would have to hitch a ride and find his own way back to the States from his deployed location, Multinational Base Tarin Kowt, Afghanistan. His anxiety about possibly missing this meaningful event raised his blood pressure to the point that blood vessels in his eyes burst.

He made it to the passenger terminal in Kandahar but was having difficulty finding a flight to Kuwait, where he could get a commercial flight back to the US. Fortunately, he encountered a group of special operation soldiers out of Hunter Army Airfield in Savannah, Georgia. They were headed home and heard that Matt was trying to get back to the US and why. They ripped off Matt's unit patch and told him he could be their chaplain for the duration of the trip back to their home base. All he had to do was pray over their flight home. Even more amazing is that Hunter, their destination, was only thirty minutes from our house. They would be flying in a C-17. He told me how great it was to sleep under the Black Hawk helicopter in the belly of the plane knowing he was finally coming home and on time for the event. He will forever be grateful for the guys who snatched him up. They had a part in changing our lives and our story. During a time when Matt wrestled with difficult leadership, it renewed our faith in the community we were called to serve.

I imagined Matt's relief as he lay on the deck of the plane, trying to sleep and reset his clock to the deafening sound of the C-17, anticipating being in my arms again. There was no way I could go back in time and experience those moments with him. But at this moment, I could see it, smell it, and feel the plane as it moved. Tears streamed down my face. I could not comprehend how Matt's heart was gripped in his chest, but I could try.

That was what mattered. I could try, and maybe love him more fully because I tried.

This revelation gave me the courage I needed to find out what else I had not understood. I got up again, and this time I walked around and talked to the crew. I asked them what they enjoyed about their job and what family members didn't understand. They talked about getting to see the world and being part of important events. Many of them had traveled on VIP flights before and felt honored to be chosen.

They said their mission often requires more energy, mentally and physically, than they felt their families understood. It was a tough job, requiring them to be ready at a moment's notice. When they got home, many family members wanted to engage and talk about their day or hear information about their trip. They all agreed that they needed at least a day to recover before they were ready to fully engage. It was tough to balance family and relationships with this kind of job. A couple of them had relationships with other service members, hoping they would understand, but sometimes the job still got in the way. Two of the young crew members were already divorced.

One of the crew members I met was a maintainer, responsible for mechanical issues as they arose. Much of his job happened before and after the flights of the day. Up early, and staying late, he was the point person to make sure the plane was fully operational for each mission. I expressed my gratitude to him for all he did to ensure our flight was safe. Earlier in the day, he had changed a tire on the aircraft. I'm not exactly sure how that is done on a C-17. He shrugged it off, but said that sometimes family doesn't comprehend the job.

"There are only so many times you can tell them that you fixed a tire or a worked on a wire," he said, "but it is the difference between the mission succeeding or not."

I was beginning to appreciate the moving parts of a mission. I thought of what it feels like as a spouse to hear the dynamics of my husband's day. There are some things we don't talk about to maintain the confidentiality of the conversations he has with soldiers. But the daily routine can easily become mundane for both of us.

I was recognizing a correlation in the intricate connection

we have as family members to the mission. We are often told that our support is paramount to success, but we don't often see how this is true. These crewman affirmed that a family's understanding of what they do, as well as their respect for the work they do, truly matters.

After making the rounds to speak with the crew, I sat back down and thought about Matt's stressful redeployment after his first deployment. I imagined what he may have needed when he came home. I wondered if I had given him enough time to decompress. I reflected on our reintegration. The second deployment was much easier, as he was able to return early.

The first was a full year, filled with major life-changing experiences for both of us. When he came home, I was anxious to resume normal life.

Mentors cautioned me there would be a new normal. I thought this meant that our schedules would be off, and I would need to consider how loud noises and crowded rooms might impact him. While this was true, I didn't realize our relationship and connection would have to go through a period of reconstruction.

Like many military spouses, I had become independent and confident over the course of that year. At the start, I struggled with smaller decisions. By the end, the boys and I had a routine, and I had a way of making decisions, even major ones. I didn't bother Matt with most of them. I could handle just about anything that came my way. Without realizing it, and out of my need to survive, I had learned to live without him.

He had been without the physical touch of his wife and children for a year. His longing to feel connected to us was more than just about hugs and affection. He needed a safe place to be himself. He needed to rejoin his family where he belonged. He needed a place to rest physically, emotionally, spiritually, and socially. The trauma and death he experienced affected him in many ways, including valuing life more than ever. He came home with a *carpe diem* mindset. His values shifted toward family, relationships, and living life to the fullest, while mine had become control- and responsibility-driven.

Ultimately, these outlooks clashed. I wanted him to know he has a place in our home and family, but I had grown accustomed to doing things my way. Although I valued having a full life, I couldn't figure out how to experience life fully at his level. Getting to know each other again and learning to live in sync took time. Even though I had grown accustomed to having control, I was exhausted from being the sole parent. I was ready to rest and have us function as a team again. I waited for his sleep schedule to adjust. I waited until the reintegration meetings over the first two weeks concluded. But then, the military began telling family members not to move too quickly or do anything that might upset our soldiers. I was told in meetings to be mindful of how he might have changed. In honor of that, I didn't bring up what I was feeling or many of my own needs. As I pushed them down, I continued to run on empty.

Matt said he came home to an angry wife, and I defended myself for years. Now, I could look back and see that I *was* angry. I didn't think I was angry at him, because it wasn't his fault that he came home changed by war. I couldn't blame the military, because we were the ones who signed up. I had no one to blame and nowhere to place my anger, so I harbored it. I was angry that our life was different, that we couldn't mindlessly walk through the mall, that when eating in any restaurant, Matt had to sit at a table with a clear line of vision to the door.

Now as the C-17 pushed through the sky, I thought about what it must have been like for Matt to come home to me that way. The day he came home, instead of a day off, we went to our son's elementary school field day. I presumed he would want to participate in things he had missed. But he needed time. What he also needed was for me to have taken care of my feelings in a healthy way by finding the support I needed, having a mentor to talk to, and educating myself on how we could move through the transition together. I thought I was strong enough to do it on my own, but I wasn't.

I could look back now and see that I was blinded by the fog of confusion about the changes in our life together. My goal with this new journey was to put aside my own stuff and see Matt's perspective more clearly. Doing so, I was seeing myself soberly, the way he saw me. I now understood what he had tried to tell me.

FULL CIRCLE

As we prepared to touch down at Baghdad International Airport, often called BIAP, I wondered if the country would look like a desert with sand from horizon to horizon. Matt had not been to Iraq, but several of our friends who deployed to Iraq called it "the sandbox." I watched the security crew at the back of the plane open a trunk with their gear and weapons. They donned bulletproof vests and armor plates and loaded their weapons. I had seen armed soldiers on post before—guarding the gate and marching in formation. I suppose I hadn't thought much about whether their weapons were loaded or not. Seeing the process of putting ammunition into these weapons was a dose of reality. I wasn't afraid exactly, but it clearly illustrated that we were in the Middle East, where our military members traveled armed and ready.

Once we were off the plane, troops in full gear accompanied us as we walked toward buildings surrounded by large concrete walls about fifteen feet high. We were directed through a fenced gate toward a small, white, one-story building. A helicopter landed nearby as we entered through the gate.

Inside the building was a small room that apparently served as a passenger terminal, which I surmised by seeing X-ray machines and metal detectors. A couple of soldiers in full kit, who had been in the helicopter that just landed, came in behind us. Some staff members greeted one soldier warmly as he took off his helmet, revealing gray hair. They were obviously glad to see him and handed him a bag of goodies brought from the States.

The original plan, for our entire group to travel by helicopter to another location in Iraq, was scuttled by heavy fog that morning. We were grounded in Baghdad.

As the group moved from the security area in the airport, a staff member indicated that I should follow him. Part of the group exited one way. I followed the staffer and the other group, including Secretary Carter, another way. We walked through a gravel alley lined with the same tall concrete barriers I'd seen earlier. The presence of so many walls created the illusion of a life-sized maze. On the five-minute walk, I chatted with various people. The first stop was a private meeting for the secretary, and a security member asked if I was press.

As it was only the second day, I wasn't sure of my place. I looked around and saw no other press with us before answering, "Kinda."

I was a military spouse trying to understand what deployment was like. If I had the opportunity to talk with troops, I wasn't going to interview them as though I were a reporter. Already at times, the secretary's staff pulled me into opportunities to see things I might not get to see if I had been strictly a member of the press. But as it turned out, I wasn't supposed to be in that particular location at that particular time.

However, being in the wrong place at the wrong time provided me with my first opportunity to speak with a US service member stationed in Iraq, who walked me back to where the press group was waiting. Although he wore civilian clothes, he was active duty, tasked to provide security that day. I found out he was unmarried and loved his job in Iraq. We talked about how family members have a hard time understanding how someone can love a job that is so far away, particularly in a place like Iraq. He chose this work because it was what he loved but the tempo was demanding, he said, making it very difficult for him to build a family. In fact, he said many of the security guys there were single.

Noting the concrete walls and gravel as we walked, I told him how my husband had described deployment as a colorless place. The soldier agreed that being in a colorless place for so long can make coming home to America feel overwhelming.

Matt often referred to deployment as "bizarro-world," where everything is different from normal life. There are so many experiences that would typically not happen in America. When he came home, those differences were hard to describe and also hard for family to comprehend. Some things I'd rather not comprehend. To this day I refuse to do a Google search for camel spiders. From the stories Matt shared, that is truly an image I never want in my mind.

June 2009—Afghanistan

There are very few days that go by where I don't feel like I am in bizarro-world. Maybe it is seeing the size of the spiders or hornets out here that look like they feast on livestock and steroids, or maybe it's accepting that I live right next to a very busy helicopter landing zone and very loud gun line. You could be going right along with your day, and then *blam* goes the test-fire of the howitzer. And you are quickly reminded that you aren't in Colorado anymore. And oddly enough, I kind of smile, because I have never really liked the status quo, and here it is anything but.

The opportunity to jump in and help dig a trash-burning pit or level some ground with a shovel, to help carry the fuel containers, or watch a hillside in the middle of the night with those on guard—those are really the moments I live for, when you feel like you are a part of this humongous system called the Army. But this past visit to OP Mustang was exceptionally interesting, because we bought a sheep to grill.
~Matt

I joined the press in a small room off to the side where they were sitting on sofas and chairs in a circle talking with the gray-haired soldier who'd come in from the helicopter. He had taken off his gear. He had dip in his mouth and a cup to spit in. He spoke to the press while their tape recorders pointed toward his face or lay on the coffee table between them. I took a seat at a conference table behind the press circle.

The soldier was Colonel Steve Warren, a spokesman for Operation Inherent Resolve. His background was public affairs. I later learned he'd spent time in the Pentagon where many of the staff and this press group had developed a strong working relationship with him. I listened as he described the current issues our troops were facing in Iraq.

Two significant cities in Iraq, Ramadi and Mosul, had been captured by the Islamic State. The Iraqi army was preparing to take back Ramadi. If they succeeded, it would be a significant win for Iraqi forces. The prime minister, though, had declined the Pentagon's offers of advisers and Apache helicopters to provide low air support to Iraqi troops to aid in taking back the city. Colonel Warren explained that accepting US support would put Prime Minister Haider al-Abadi in a difficult spot with his political rivals. Secretary Carter wanted to make it clear in his meeting with Abadi later that day that nothing would be done without the approval of the sovereign Iraqi government.

After the press had the information they needed to write about the secretary's upcoming meeting with the Iraqi prime minister, they began their work. Warren stayed in the room to answer questions for the journalists as they began writing their stories.

The situation in Iraq was complicated. We had heard the secretary's request for coalition support in Turkey, but now that we were in Iraq, we were looking at the fight from a different angle. Warren talked to the press about the dynamics of war to help them fully understand the American military perspective on what was happening in Iraq.

I liked learning what was happening in Iraq and watching how news stories are researched and written. Thus came another realization of how little I knew about the fight against terrorism and our role as a military force. I was embarrassed as a military spouse that I had not paid better attention and educated myself more about world affairs. However, I didn't want to be too hard on myself; after all, the journalists were working hard to understand the dynamics as well. Still, I felt I should have understood more. My family's life revolved around these dynamics. At a moment's notice, our life could change and Matt could be in the middle of it all. I was interested to learn about military strategy. Previously, I'd been fairly neutral in my opinions of our country's efforts in Iraq. Being there made me more aware that troops were sacrificing their lives to be part of this mission not far from where I sat. The state of Iraq mattered more to me now.

Warren took us over to the DFAC for lunch and we walked into a huge cafeteria that appeared populated by members of every branch of service and career field imaginable: Special Forces operators, soldiers, airmen, Marines, and many uniforms I didn't recognize. Our little group received a lot of strange looks as we walked through the buffet lines. There was a section labeled "healthy food" that looked surprisingly unhealthy, an American section, various ethnic offerings, and a wide variety of desserts, even ice cream. All drinks, including water, were bottled.

I asked Warren about the service members in uniforms I didn't recognize. He explained there were eighteen different coalition groups in Baghdad. I hadn't realized so many countries were involved. After what I saw in Turkey the day before, and now this, the world felt even more integrated.

After lunch, we returned to the press room where we had Wi-Fi. I replied to tweets and waited for America to wake up. Even though the fog caused us to miss out on the trip by helicopter, it was nice to have connectivity for the day.

As with every stop, the defense secretary had plans to speak to the troops. But the visit by helicopter to see the prime minister to discuss the role of American troops and support in Iraq delayed him. While the troops waited in an outdoor seating area for his arrival, I wanted to talk to some of them about their experiences. When I saw a couple of female soldiers on the side, I approached them. I told them who I was and asked if I could chat with them. Soon we were joking and giggling. They talked about their sweethearts back home.

Since Christmas was only a couple of weeks away, I asked about care packages. I had always struggled with what to send Matt. Often he said he couldn't think of anything he needed, so I filled his boxes with anything I thought would remind him of home. After five or six boxes, though, I ran out of ideas.

The women shared how minimally they lived there, agreeing that "There is nothing we need." Matt used to tell me the same thing.

The women said people were very sweet to send them things from home, but they simply had no room for extra personal items. They explained that they slept in cots arranged like bunk beds, leaving little room for personal space. I envisioned bunk beds like the ones my sons slept in.

"We feel bad because we end up having to give away a lot of things or throw them away. We have nowhere to put things."

I thought that sounded awful, but they countered by saying they were quite content with just the necessities. When I explained the frustration that family back home has wanting to send something to make deployment easier, the women reiterated that they really didn't need anyone to make it easier for them. They were not miserable and they felt content with what they had.

I remembered a time shortly after Matt and I were married when we had very little money. I was quite content with our new beginning. We had everything we needed but not the luxury of weekly shopping trips for extras at the mall. I remember feeling tempted to subscribe to a fashion magazine but deciding against it. I knew looking at that magazine would only make me feel discontented and long for things I couldn't have. In a way, I shut off my thoughts about desiring more than what I had already. I never felt I was missing out. I asked the women if it was possible that living minimally made it easier to shut off their wants for more.

They appeared surprised at the thought, but then agreed. They had come to a mind-set where they were grateful for what they had. If they truly needed anything, they could order it online, but some possessions were simply not realistic in Iraq.

The women said healthy food was far more appreciated than lots of junk food. Disposable toiletries and nice-smelling soaps from home were also nice. These consumable supplies don't take up much valuable space. They added that although they wouldn't be able to see family for Christmas, other troops here had become like family. Pointing to the soldiers gathered, one woman said, "We will have bonfires and talk, and it will be everything we need."

I thanked them for their time just as Secretary Carter arrived to address the group.

Christmas 2009—Afghanistan

> *Hello Love,*
> *So SGT Rackley walks into the office with a bundt fruit-cake. Not your store-bought, shelf-preserved fruitcake. No. One that someone lovingly bought embalmed and unnaturally colored cherries to make. I could both hug and punch*

him, because this is definitely going to ruin my healthy eating this week. Yes, I love fruitcake so much that I don't have the will power to resist it, and I don't care who knows. Give me your tired, your poor ... your fruitcakes. Sounds like a motto for the nut house, eh?

Sharing.

And we just came back from Pirtle-King where we barged into all the barracks and handed out stockings filled with all the goodies that folks back home have shared with soldiers they will never know by name. And they laughed and smiled and shared the various and sundry fillings of their stockings, and traded among themselves when they saw their buddy pull out one of their favorite things from their stocking. And they were happy. And they poured out the contents into shared boxes in the room where everyone could come by and pick out candy or snacks whenever they wanted.

Sharing.

I love that soldiers share, they share in the cold, sleepless nights of being on guard and will go keep their brothers company when it isn't even their shift and they could be sleeping. And they all jump in to help with details like filling sandbags or cleaning something when they see their brother sweating and struggling, because there is something in them that will not let them watch their brother bear the burden alone. I wish that it were a characteristic of all humanity, it just isn't, but that isn't to say that it isn't the way God intended it to be.

Love,

Matthew

Before we left Baghdad that day, there was a press gaggle where the secretary updated us on new details from his meeting with the Iraqi prime minister. After listening to Warren earlier in the day, the press gaggle made more sense. Earlier in the day, the press had gathered information they needed to get the story; the gaggle was for any updates or changes that developed while the secretary met with foreign leaders.

Each night, new articles went back to America about what was happening in the region. I felt strange being in the middle of world events and seeing them simplified into quick sound bites and news stories that may or may not be read.

When it was time to leave, I wished I had seen more of Baghdad, but I did not leave disappointed because—well—I went to Baghdad. We boarded the C-17 and I buckled in. I settled in to relax my brain from all I'd taken in.

Just when I thought the day couldn't hold any more new revelations, a pilot walked up to me, knelt down, and over the roaring of the engines, asked if I wanted to see the cockpit. I jumped at the opportunity. I followed him to the front and climbed the spiral staircase at the top front of the plane. When I reached the top, I could see a pilot and copilot flying the plane. Behind the main cockpit was a small space where a set of bunks was built into the wall for pilots who were not flying to get some sleep. Three other crew members were waiting for me.

"So we heard that you are a military spouse hoping to talk to some of us who are married," said the pilot who brought me there. "What would you like to know?"

I was floored by these crew members' openness and willingness to talk. I explained to them my goal and asked what they felt spouses didn't understand about deployment or trips like these. The one who spoke first mentioned that the jet lag of flying through time zones is tough to understand without experiencing it. I agreed, now that I was going through it myself; at points through the day, the ground felt unsteady as if I were on a ship.

They laughed and told me that was indeed part of the exhaustion of jet lag.

One said he was getting ready to retire and looked forward to traveling with his wife. The others laughed and added it would be good for her to experience it herself. I made an internal assumption that since he had flown all over the world, she was ready for her turn. I knew that feeling, too.

I had often said, "I don't want to deploy to a combat zone, but I'm sometimes jealous that you get to travel and see the world."

Matt usually responded with, "How about I send you to the middle of nowhere, with no shower for weeks, people shooting at you, and let you wake up in your tent to spiders the size of your fist?"

I usually rolled my eyes at him.

When I'd said the same thing to my dad about his flights to amazing destinations, he reminded me that, along with the opportunity of seeing new places, flying there was the equivalent of sitting in a coat closet for sixteen straight hours.

Seeing the small place where the pilots spent a majority of their time, I could imagine some of it becoming tiring. The other pilots agreed that they would love to bring their wives with them someday, to let them experience the fatigue and the rest they needed afterward. They were not trying to be snide, but they wished their wives had a better understanding and an accurate picture of their duties.

I asked if any of them had children. Several did, and it seemed as though the small space became smaller as it grew quieter. The one soon retiring pointed to the "AMC" Air Mobility Command patch on his chest and joked that it actually stood for "Another Missed Christmas."

The pain of leaving family behind, even to do what they loved to do, was palpable. The pilots talked of loving their spouses even more for all they do back at home while they are gone. One said he had missed all his kids' birthdays. Another described how much his teenagers love to tell other kids what their dad does for a living.

He said the kids wait until all the other kids at the lunch table start talking about what their parents do for a living.

"My dad is a doctor."

"My dad is a lawyer."

When his teen spoke, he said, she would share what he did and motion with her hands a mic drop.

His kids understood an element of the cool factor he had fallen in love with. The proud father looked down and kicked the toe of his boot. This was his calling, and the gleam in his eye made that obvious. As I listened and watched them standing there with their arms folded across their chests as if guarding their hearts and looking at the floor, I saw my dad.

So many times he stood in front of me, wanting me to understand how he could hold both the calling in his life and his love for me at the same time. I didn't fully understand that about him until this moment. I could now see why he loved flying so much. He was a great father, there for me even when he was jet-lagged. In fact, I don't think I ever saw him tired. Maybe he hid it from me.

Dad made every effort to come to my track meets, timing me with his stopwatch and yelling for me to beat my personal record. He provided everything I needed and yet taught me to work for the extras in life. When he flew for Delta, he would call me at college and invite me for an impromptu trip to wherever he was going, promising to have me back in time for class. We visited Montana and drove the open highways, tubed down a river in Arizona, and went several other places.

He was available when he was available. He was and is a good man. Even now, as he worked tirelessly alongside Matt at our new home in Virginia, I was thankful for the integrity that life and the military had instilled in him. He had become my friend, too, someone I could call when military life made me frustrated, when I wondered if I was ruining my kids. He always offered seasoned advice and wisdom with the big picture in mind, but never answered decisions I needed to make for myself. We already had a great relationship; but in this moment, I understood him in a new way. Who he was and is in my life is what matters, not how often he has been physically present.

Matt and I sometimes struggle with the guilt of dragging our kids along on this crazy life, but my father's example reminds us that our job is to raise them well. Part of that job includes showing them what it looks like to follow a calling.

Standing in this sacred circle of pilots as we flew over the Gulf waters in darkness, I told them about my dad who was also an Air Force pilot who missed birthdays and Christmas. I told them that as a child I used to wonder if he loved flying more than he loved me.

"Now that I am an adult, I have an awesome relationship with my dad," I said. "You know why? Because he is a good man. He always did what was right. He continued to set the example of following his calling. Because he did, he taught me to do the same. I am standing here right now because I am called to something. As hard as it was to leave my family, I knew I was called to be here right now. My father's example showed me that it is who you are that your kids will remember, not how many holidays you missed."

They nodded in silence. I hoped my words made a difference. I hoped they were words my dad would have appreciated hearing years ago, words I looked forward to saying to him when I got home.

One of the pilots mentioned how glad he was that he would be home for Christmas this time. The crew in the plane behind us would not. On a mission that includes a VIP like the secretary of defense, the pilots explained, another C-17 flies ten minutes behind in case backup is needed. When the E-4B is in the air, it is accompanied by two fuel tankers and a C-17.

"This is a no-fail mission," said one. "There is backup for everything."

They talked about how much they loved the satisfaction of finishing a mission successfully.

The pilot who brought me up to the cockpit emphasized to me how much he appreciated his wife. He said he didn't know how she was able to be so strong at home with the kids, and that he couldn't do it. He thanked me for what I was doing for spouses and that we have the hardest job.

"Thank you," I said. "Why don't we agree that what you do is difficult, too, and that she likely couldn't do what you do? When a military couple is at their best for each other, what you get is a powerful team."

The green lights inside the cockpit glowed, but the sky outside was dark. The crew gave me a helmet, a headset (so I could listen to the pilots talking to each other during the flight), and a pair of night-vision goggles. The equipment was heavy and clunky and made me into a bobblehead trying to hold up the weight. But the view was worth it. Matt had told me about the power of NVGs and had even sent me videos from his deployment, but now I saw through them with my own eyes. Through NVGs, the night sky glowed a magnificent clear green. I could see every detail of each cloud beneath us as if it were daytime, and I could make out ships in the waters below.

In the distance, I saw the lights of Saudi Arabia. The Bahraini airport was already making contact, and we began our descent. Time for me to return to my seat—but I had one more question. I asked the pilot who had been my guide to tell me the most beautiful thing he anticipated seeing out the cockpit window when he flew. I expected him to mention rainbows or sunsets, maybe the incredible view I had just seen with the NVGs. I thought he might describe the aurora borealis or maybe a distant thunderstorm. But he paused, gave a thoughtful "*Hmmm,*" and looked out the window.

"Home," he said.

December 16, 2015—Virginia/Matt's Facebook Post

>*In between trying to hang the right pictures where I believe Corie would want them, I paused to see if she had uploaded something on Twitter. She is out and about, and I cannot reach out to her, call, or text. I have to wait for her to land wherever she will find herself, or to be finished with the mission today. Spouses, I now fully understand having to sit back and wait to hear from your service member. Wondering how their day went, where they are, or what they experienced. So much of our marriages are built on what we experience together, shared memories. Though I know that after this trip is complete, Corie and I will have a shared experience that has been years apart. The sounds, the smells, and the dismal sights.*

>*And I found her Day 2 blog and read through it. I watched her video yesterday and cried at parts. Veterans feel so misunderstood. Our experiences exist in a world that 99.9 percent of Americans will not experience, and when we try to paint the picture, it takes too much time. So we choose a life of separation and confusion. Our lives changed by something others cannot fathom.*

>*As I finished the blog, I flipped through her pictures standing beside or inside a C-17. Looking at her, arm-in-arm with female 10th Mountain Division soldiers with concrete T-walls behind her, my heart exclaimed, "You're Doing It! You. Are. Doing. It!"*

>*It has not been easy to get here, for her, for us. Finishing the Career Course, getting ready to move, preparing for the trip, planning every detail, and keeping it secret from everyone. But like a proud parent watching a child walk again, or for the first time, knowing how hard they have struggled to get here and yet how hard it is to walk through this experience. It is not easy, it is not simple.*

>*But, Love, You're Doing It.*

>*~Matthew*

EMBRACING THE SUCK

I woke up in a panic. It was light outside. Did I oversleep? I ran to my phone and relief swept over me when I realized it was still a few minutes before my alarm would go off. I had slept a solid seven-and-a-half hours. I felt great. Perhaps this was the end of the jet lag? Another example of my naivety.

The day's schedule was sent by email or slipped under the doors of our hotel rooms each day. Only then did we know for sure where we were going. Our schedule said Erbil, Iraq. I had never heard of Erbil, Iraq. I thought, *Isn't that something every military spouse should know?*

I wish I could have done more research about potential stops on our itinerary. But not knowing where we were going until the night before made that difficult. I had to get ready, pack for the day and check the previous night's uploads on social media. Once I left the hotel, I couldn't count on access to Wi-Fi. There might be windows of opportunity or not. I had enough time to grab a quick breakfast and head to the lobby to meet the group for departure.

Each day's activities had a rhythm. We'd rush from the hotel to the plane, land, and sync up with key military leaders, then split up into the press group and the official group, which included the secretary and his staff. While the secretary was privately briefed by military leaders or met with leaders of other countries, the press was typically briefed by a military spokesperson about events in the region.

That day I was given an opportunity to talk with female troops and see their living conditions. A lunch was planned with about fifteen female soldiers, so we could have a candid discussion about what deployment was like for them. The meeting was closed to the press.

At first, not being a soldier made me feel like I didn't quite fit in, but after introducing myself, I felt I was somehow an extension from home, a connection. I remember when Matt's best friend came home from Afghanistan on leave. He and his wife stopped by so I could give him something to take back to Matt. I wanted so badly to hug Matt's friend. Not because I needed a hug from him, but because he'd been next to Matt just days before, and I hadn't touched Matt in more than six months. It seemed that if I hugged his friend, it would be the closest I could get to Matt—like I could somehow reach Afghanistan through his friend. A couple of the female soldiers looked at me the same way I must have looked at Matt's friend, as though I could be a connection to those they loved. Some were spouses of active duty members, as well as being active duty themselves.

The most personally enlightening part of the day was getting to see the living conditions of the soldiers in Erbil. They were rougher than I expected, providing the necessities but no frills.

Hundreds of tents were arranged in rows of ten or more, each one very close to the next. They were khaki-colored, nearly the shade of the surrounding gravel. The camouflage netting draped over them offered a slight contrast. I wondered if people could hear from other tents at night when it was quiet. I imagined soldiers calling from tent to tent, joking, laughing, or complaining, using words I probably shouldn't write here.

I was given a tour of one of the sleeping tents. It was about twenty feet long and had one air vent in the front. Sleepers in the front would get too much air, while those in the back would get too little. The major giving the tour said the strong smell of peppermint was intended to deter mice. Snakes were another problem. A sign on the inside of the door had a lot of exclamation points: "Do NOT turn off the air conditioner anytime! A warm tent invites poisonous snakes and rats!!!!"

The bunks were more like cots, definitely not like the ones my boys slept in. The top bed was only chest high, so the sleeper on the bottom level would have to roll to get out of the bunk.

I now understood what the female soldiers in Baghdad said the day before about having no room to spare. The only space each person could call her own was a cot. Anything extra had to go under it or hang on it, I guessed. The major told us how excited she was to get a bath mat from her family, so she could wake up and put her feet on something soft in the morning rather than the cold hard floor covered in a tarp.

I pictured Matt living in some of these conditions.

January 4, 2010—Afghanistan

> *Hey Love,*
> *Still at Bari Alai, won't get back tonight. Just relaxing and trying to sleep on a very uncomfortable cot. I am thinking that for my birthday, I want a nice, fashionable Lazy Boy-like recliner. Not one of those puffy ones, something sleek and stylish, you know? After spending a year sitting on plywood, cots, small camping chairs, rocks, ammo cans and the like ... I think I might really like one of those, and you can use it, too.*
> *All my love, I miss you!*
> *Matthew*

The tents were raised on plywood platforms a few inches above the gravel. Matt had mentioned gravel being everywhere—how he had to get dressed and fully kit up just to go to the bathroom. I saw the gravel in Turkey and Baghdad, but here I saw even more covering the ground beneath and between the tents, bathroom facilities, the DFAC. This was not small pebbles or crushed gypsum, but more like small rocks. Only two or three of them would fit in the palm of my hand. I looked at the tents, the gravel, and the distance, and imagined Matt navigating it at night and in all kinds of weather.

A soldier ran by, trying to get in some PT. I admired the determination needed to run on that surface. I gave thanks that Matt had urged me to buy the boots I wore on this trip.

June 22, 2009—Afghanistan

> *Hi Love,*
> *We are located right across from the DFAC, so we will have plenty of visibility and centrality for folks to stop by, relax, and enjoy things together. Everywhere here is covered in large, fist-sized rocks of gravel to keep the dust down, so I now have Gumby ankles. You can't really walk*

*anywhere without looking a little clumsy, and I would hate
to try and run somewhere. Everybody is starting to wear
down just a little bit, you don't realize what working seven
days a week will do to you after a while.*

  Love,
  Matthew

I knew that bathrooms varied widely from place to place.
In a few places Matt stayed, troops took turns burning their
excrement. The women's bathrooms at Erbil were nicer than
I expected, with stalls separated by curtains. The main restrooms had been recently updated. The staff who had been here
before mentioned the improvements, but the walls separating
the men's and women's restrooms didn't even go to the ceiling.
Sounds and smells traveled freely.

At the next stop on our tour, the mail room, we were greeted
with smiles. I could see why Matt talked about this as a happy
place. Who doesn't love a package or letter from home? As it
was mid-December, the mail room was decorated with battery-
operated Christmas lights and other festive decorations. Three
soldiers stood behind a makeshift plywood desk in front of
shelves with racks of stored weapons. I expected soldiers to be
carrying their weapons. I was prepared to see everyone with
weapons on all the time. So I asked.

The major explained that because of their work with Kurdish coalition forces at that location, they only carried concealed
weapons and stored the others. She lifted her ACU blouse to
show me her hand gun. I took that to mean that packing heat
discreetly makes for a nicer work environment.

I asked the guys behind the mailroom counter what they
felt spouses didn't understand about what they do during deployment. One said he thought he was safer here than his wife
was back home in Baltimore. He said that many family members think that because they are deployed to Iraq, they are
immediately and constantly in danger. He said he felt extremely
safe and wished his family could believe he was.

I understood this. Telling my mom and Matt's mom about
making this trip brought them both to tears. Just entering an
area synonymous with conflict makes family members assume
the worst. During Matt's second deployment to Afghanistan, I

think he stopped trying to convince me he was safe. Maybe I just stopped saying I was worried. But I was.

Back in the mailroom, another soldier said he was the one who couldn't understand how his wife managed. "She's the one home with three small children," he said. "I feel like I have time to relax, and she doesn't get that. You guys have the hardest job, not us."

I heard that message a lot from those I spoke with. At first, I thought they were just saying those things to be nice or out of guilt for leaving their families, but I was beginning to believe they actually did see their spouses' jobs as harder than their own. I appreciated their reassurance very much and politely received it on behalf of their spouses.

Deep down, I knew that every couple needs to recognize each other's struggles instead of trying to decide who has a harder job or whose experience is worse or more difficult. Each is totally different from the other, requiring every bit from each person. We are dependent on each other for success.

I was impressed with the facilities I saw at Erbil. Not every service member was in such an established place. When Matt told me that the operating room at Bostick was actually in a tent like those I saw that day, I had a clear picture of those conditions.

"Embrace the suck" is a phrase Matt often used to describe less-than-ideal conditions or circumstances. There was no way I had to embrace the suck at any point during this trip, but everything I was seeing and hearing made a difference for me.

August 31, 2009—Afghanistan

> *Hi Love,*
>
> *For most of us here, we are as content as we have ever been, minus the emptiness of missing family. But so that you may understand how far-reaching your gifts have been on the other side of the world, I will give as appropriate a picture as I can. We don't have a PX, which is the Walmart of military installations. That may sound inconsequential, but imagine not being able to go buy anything you want, ever. Just make a request to someone on the other side of the world, and wait. Wait for the unpredictable helicopter flights to bring it to you. Yeah, I know that birds only fly up*

there six days out of the month and the last two flights to deliver mail were canceled, but just wait. I promise it will be there ... someday. There is no other way to build patience and contentment than to remove from you all control over what you get and when it arrives. Amazing.

Also, some of our places have hot chow once a day. So if you want something fresh-cooked rather than out of a three-year-old, well-preserved brown plastic pouch, you best go ahead and wake up at 0400, because that's when we eat around here. Any later and it is not a sound idea. So you develop an uncanny appreciation to be content with what you are given, whenever it happens to arrive. You make the best of it and always pass the hot sauce and salt.

And then there's the lack of showers at some places. I mean, yeah, there's a "shower building," but between guard shifts and details and eating and trying to catch up with loved ones on the phone or internet ... you can't muster the motivation to drag six liters of water to the top of the shower building to put in the tank, which doesn't sound appealing because you forgot to put it out in the sun to warm up. Baby wipes and Gold Bond can work for one more day, eh?

Yet in the midst of what we like to term, "the Suck," we laugh and crack up. We jibe one another and find a few moments to take each other's money at cards. We watch pirated copies of movies that have just been released in the theaters wishing the guy with the video camera had stayed still or not laughed during that part. We start to remember food that we can't wait to order.

But the best part of it all is when you get that package from home, or someone, anyone, and you slice it open with the knife from your Gerber to reveal something from the other side of the world. Something that someone took the initiative to send to you. Maybe they know you and know what you like, or maybe they just thought this or that might make it all a little bit better in the long run.

We had some soldiers from 10th Mountain Division, Fort Drum, come back through our Forward Operating Base a month or so ago, coming back from the 11th day of a 72-hour mission. Yeah that happens sometimes. They were disheveled and dirty, grimy and borrowing some of our ACU tops, because ours didn't have blood stains on them. And I invited them into the chapel to take as much of the hygiene *supplies as they needed to get a shower and shave, and it became Christmas morning in July. All because of what folks had sent.*

You never know who that small bottle of shampoo, or pack of ramen noodles will help. Sometimes that package of cookies or jar of peanut butter becomes the only reminder that this too shall pass. It is a reminder that there is a civilized world out there that appreciates the sacrifice that we and our families are making. We are all someone's son or daughter, someone's brother or sister, someone's husband or wife, someone's father or mother. And we fight so that they do not have to. Like any normal person we become discouraged when we evac one of our own, or the mission does not fully go according to plan, which it never does. We adjust our future based on what happens echelons above us, and we "Charlie Mike" (continue mission). And for all of its faults, we secretly love it all.

~Matthew

Embracing the suck for an extended amount of time would surely change a person—even add character to those in a Western culture who are used to entitlement and convenience. Matt rarely grumbles at the minimal amount of civilian clothes he has in our closet. He is anxious to get rid of clutter whenever we move. He continually reminds the boys of the heaping amount of blessings they call the Toy Room. While many of us can feel frustrated by a service member's minimalist attitude, it is a reminder that they know something we haven't learned. Perhaps they can teach us a lot.

It was time for me to join the press group again in the main building in a room with rows of tables and chairs, like a briefing room. Journalists took turns passing around a Wi-Fi hotspot, trying to send in their articles on a US deadline. Colonel Warren had been flown in again and was in the room describing new developments. I now looked forward to these briefings.

Secretary Carter was meeting in Erbil with Masoud Barzani, president of the Kurdistan Region, offering him enough equipment to arm two brigades of Kurds who were ready to help with the battle for Mosul. Islamic State terrorists had launched an attack against Kurdish forces as an offensive tactic to protect Mosul, but with the help of US advisers and air support for the Kurds, they were repelled.

As I sat back and watched the journalists work together to gather the facts, I thought about the importance of their job. Like the rest of American citizens, military spouses are dependent on the news to find out what is going on in the world and to help us make sense of where our service members go and why. I did the best I could to make sense of the information I heard and was incredibly grateful for the press doing the work for me.

This hardworking group had also left spouses, children, and other family to be here. I watched as they dove into finding information they needed for the day, asked all the right questions to fully educate themselves, and then spent whatever creative energy they had left writing their reports so that Americans could learn about what we saw each day and hopefully spend more than thirty seconds digesting it.

I checked out often when Matt tried to educate me on the Middle East and the War on Terror. I assumed it was too complicated or overwhelming for me to take in. I now saw how wrong I was. I could see how everything worked together and how my own soldier played a part in the overall mission. I owed it to both of us to understand why he was being sent wherever the mission called.

Watching the news being gathered and distilled also gave me greater appreciation for the complexity of the issues. Military members, once they come home, can respond differently to the casual or impulsive opinions of others on war and military efforts that they hear about in the news. These topics were personal for Matt, because his life and the lives of others were deeply impacted. For many service members, it's not just conversation or opinion sharing. These conflicts have cost many of their friends' lives.

Our last stop, to my surprise, was the chaplain's office. I was thrilled. From Matt's pictures of his office at Bostick, I had some idea what this one would look like. Outside the door, the Army chaplain crest was painted as a mural on the hallway wall. Entering was almost like walking into Matt's photograph. The room was warm and inviting, as a chaplain's office should be. There was a rug on the floor and a large American flag on the wall behind the desk. Chairs were arranged in a circle for us. Christmas lights twinkled and Christmas music played in the background.

The chaplain greeted us with a smile and offered us authentic Kurdish desserts. He had brewed coffee in French presses for us. When Matt was deployed, he enjoyed serving good coffee that I sent him to share with soldiers who came for counseling or just to take a break. For the first time on this trip, it felt like Christmas to me—it felt like home. I pictured Matt there with us as we talked about what it was like for the soldiers in Erbil.

The chaplain asked if I had any questions, and strangely enough, I didn't. Feeling at home in his office, I had a good idea what his world was like and possibly his average day. I was thankful for how much Matt had decompressed his days to me over the phone or through email snapshots of his world.

This visit seemed perfectly timed in preparation for the next day when we would travel to Afghanistan. I felt my heart preparing for something that I couldn't predict. I had seen Turkey and Iraq, the sleeping and eating conditions during deployment. I'd talked with troops and now spent time in the chaplain's office. The time had come to set foot on the soil that actually changed my husband and changed us.

Before leaving the chaplain's room, we noticed a guitar in the corner. The chaplain said it belonged to his assistant. We asked if the musician might be willing to play a song for us. The chaplain left the room and returned with his assistant, who seemed slightly flustered but eager for the opportunity. He picked up the guitar, placed it on his knee, began to strum and sing:

> *Worthy is the*
> *Lamb who was slain*
> *Holy, Holy, is He*
> *Sing a new song*
> *To Him who sits on*
> *Heaven's Mercy Seat*

Tears welled in my eyes. On this day before my own trip to Afghanistan, this man who didn't know me or Matt, or our story, was singing *Revelation Song*.

MOUNTAINS OF GRIEF

April 10, 2010—Afghanistan

Only those things for which a price has been paid have lasting value and true worth.
~Matt

I had considerable work to do when I returned to the hotel, but thanks to my press colleagues I learned how to connect to a faster Internet, and my YouTube videos were uploading more speedily. I was in bed by 1:00 a.m., and we were meeting to leave for Afghanistan at 7:00 a.m. Though Matt told me not to worry about checking in, I missed him. Every day brought new epiphanies about his deployment experiences that I wanted to talk about with him. But on this day, I was on my own.

I was pushing myself every waking moment to pay attention to each detail and learn from each moment, from every sound, smell, and conversation. Exhaustion was hitting me harder each day, and I wondered how long it might be before my body shut down. I was physically tired from lack of sleep and emotionally drained from days of heightened awareness.

This day in Afghanistan would be as close as I'd ever been to where Matt was deployed. I was disappointed we were not going to J-bad and the 4ID memorial. I wore my t-shirt anyway.

Both of Matt's deployments were in Afghanistan. Despite our endless conversations about his time there, I was left feeling further from him. All his stories, so many I couldn't relate to, happened there without me. Like a thief, Afghanistan had taken pieces of Matt and didn't give them back to him, me, or our family. This was *the* place. I was about to see the mountains of Afghanistan with my own eyes.

In 2008, when we pulled up to our new home in Fort Carson,

Colorado, our first army assignment, we were moved by the magnificence of the Rocky Mountains that were practically across the street from us. We couldn't take our eyes off them. Cheyenne Mountain and Pikes Peak walled off one side of the stretch of highway that ran near Fort Carson. Those mountains became a constant in my life, immovable yet changing with the seasons. When I woke up each morning, I looked out the window to witness their shifting moods: a blanket of snow, the bright yellow of Aspens in the fall, and greens in the summer.

Even the clouds seemed to be inspired by the mountains, taking on new colors in the rising or setting sun. On some days the clouds rolled in and covered them completely. On those days it was difficult to find my bearings, because the mountains had become my reference point. Heading north, the mountains were on my left. Coming home from Colorado Springs, I knew they were on the right. After a couple of cloudy days, I found myself missing the steadfast friends that told me which direction I was going.

Matt was assigned to 3-61CAV, part of the 4th Brigade Combat Team of the 4th Infantry Division. The altitude at Fort Carson was similar to the mountains of Afghanistan where his unit was being sent. Fort Carson was a good place for soldiers to acclimate to thinner mountain air, a process which normally took at least six months. We had nine months to get used to the altitude and the military culture before our first deployment.

As we became involved with other families there, the command provided meetings to train and prepare spouses for their soldiers to leave. Those meetings in the spring of 2009 helped us put our living wills, powers of attorney, and other paperwork in order. We were warned this would be a difficult deployment, but I figured they said that to everyone.

Matt would be going to a remote Forward Operating Base called Bostick in the mountains of Afghanistan. I didn't even know what a FOB was, much less where Matt was going. He had given me a map, but just that he was going to Afghanistan was plenty for me to digest. I didn't comprehend that the region was the cause of so much concern. I didn't think I needed to understand more of the map unless it affected the address where I sent his packages.

During the months and weeks leading up to the deployment, we felt we needed to be as perfect as possible for each other and spend every moment together. The intensity and pressure, combined with the stress from individual emotions and the fear of the unknown eventually caught up with us. We only had one major fight to blow off the tension of saying goodbye for a year. Our shared underlying and unspoken question was, "What if I never see you again?"

Before Matt left, we sat down at our favorite local restaurant to work out our goals, as individuals and as a couple. We wanted to end the deployment better than we started. We coined our motto "Thrive, Don't Survive." We decided that one way we would accomplish our goal was to each be the other's "go-to person." Matt and I choose to share all the difficult or gruesome details of a deployment. Some couples instead agree ahead of time that sharing details makes the spouse at home worry or the service member unable to compartmentalize. As a chaplain, Matt knew he'd need a place to decompress after taking on the burdens of others, and as a therapist, I felt sure I could handle the details. I thought Afghanistan was a dangerous place to go in general, but I didn't think I had much to worry about. Matt had assured me he would be in safe places and he wouldn't take undue risks.

Before leaving, Matt prepped the house and cars as much as possible and tried to set me up for success. Then there was simply nothing left to do but wait. The last three hours before his departure, we stared at each other while the boys ran oblivious circles around us. Finally he stood up, held us all and said his goodbyes while holding back tears. He walked out the door, and that was it.

Like many military spouses, I didn't realize I was saying goodbye to more than just my husband. I thought the physical distance between us during that year was the most difficult thing we'd face, that keeping our relationship connected during his absence would be the biggest challenge for us to work through. Of course he would miss the boys growing up in that year, holidays, and activities we would normally do as a family, but I expected everything would be fine again once he got home. I didn't understand his job enough to anticipate what his role would look like in a deployment like this one. Neither of us anticipated the events that would unfold before he returned home. It turned out, those briefings mattered. Those maps mattered.

While Matt was at FOB Bostick, most of his troopers in 3-61CAV were spread out at various combat outposts, notably COP Keating and observation posts in austere and remote locations in the mountains of Afghanistan. Because Matt's job was to assess the morale and provide support to all his troops, he needed to go to them when they couldn't come to him. The only way to visit his soldiers was by helicopter, always at night. For safety reasons, flights were limited and what each flight carried was prioritized. First priority was ammunition and supplies. If Matt received word that he could go, he tried to send me a quick email to let me know. Depending on where he went, he might not have access to internet or phone. Sometimes I didn't hear from him for a couple of weeks, especially if he was stuck at a remote post waiting for another bird to fly him out.

June 8, 2009—Afghanistan

Hey Love,

I was going to try and call you yesterday, or drop you an email, but it ended up not happening. We have begun traveling around to the COPs and OPs, not really getting a chance to sleep and relax. We left around midnight last night, crashed for a few hours and intended to leave this COP [Keating] today, but we're stuck here until tomorrow. The major originally wanted us to stick around Bostick for a little while before beginning to make these trips, because he was afraid we would get stuck out somewhere ... which we did.

Other than that I am doing well. The scenery is beautiful; the mountains remind me of Colorado, except it is much more green here with terraced steppes to farm on. It has been cool to hop on these helicopters each night. They only fly at night up here. Anyways, I will let you know when we get back and get settled at Bostick. Tell the boys I love and miss them, and I am having the most unique birthday ever!

~Matthew

It seemed a great start at first—almost as if Matt were

getting paid to "play army." He enjoyed visiting soldiers and loved boosting morale and encouraging troops to stay connected to their families back home. Many of his hours while at FOB Bostick were spent in an operating room with Major Brad "Doc" Zagol. When there weren't enough hands in the OR, Matt helped with duties such as requesting meals for the medical staff during all-day mass casualties or performing chest compressions during CPR.

Matt spoke of those days in the surgical aid station as if they were scenes from M.A.S.H., and Doc Zagol saved lives all the time. The way he described Zagol when sharing his larger-than-life personality and skills, I pictured the doctor as a tall Samoan. In my mind, he was a giant. When I later met Zagol, I found out he was tall, but not Samoan, another example of my mistaken images of deployment. Zagol was an endearing white guy with glasses—a big-hearted man with humor to match. No wonder he and Matt got along so well. Humor was crucial to getting through tough days in the OR.

The deployment became very real, very quickly. This was not playing army. An essential part of a chaplain's mission was to be with the wounded and the dying. The first loss came a little over a month into the deployment on July 14, 2009. Sergeant First Class Jason "J-Breeze" Fabrizi had brought his platoon up from COP Pirtle-King to FOB Bostick to re-fit on the day before and spent the evening playing in a poker tournament with some of the other non-commissioned officers. He won the whole tournament that night.

Fabrizi was the first soldier to die in combat for whom Matt provided a memorial service and later counseling for his bereaved comrades. The squadron was devastated by this loss. Many more from Fabrizi's platoon were injured throughout that year, coming in and out of the aid station, raising anxiety in Afghanistan and at home.

When Tyler Parten was killed a few months later, and I heard the strain in Matt's voice on the phone, I knew the deployment would not get easier. I began to worry about the toll the year would take on Matt. He had to walk more closely with death than we had imagined. To his advantage, he comes from two generations of police officers and is innately calm and effective in moments of crisis. Medical professionals, police, and other first responders also deal with trauma and death on a daily basis.

September 26, 2009—Afghanistan

Hey Hun,

It has been a pretty slow day here, in the DFAC they served a pizza buffet with handmade pizza for lunch and we had that with some near beer, and it was almost like we weren't deployed for a minute. The pizza was pretty good and the laughs around the table were better. It is funny what things become a comfort on different days, especially after yesterday with so much counseling, and I forgot to mention that we had some guys get into contact, and the interpreter was shot through the face and I was doing chest compressions (CPR) on him while the rest of the surgeons and nurses were running IVs, pushing atropine and blood, and doing all the things like what you see on the TV. I haven't been able to watch Grey's Anatomy *here, but in a weird way I have started to live it. We even had to use the paddles on him three times, but we lost him. It hit a handful of people pretty hard, so I have tried to make rounds and make sure that they are okay.*

I don't really know what to do with experiences like that, so I just put them on the shelf and consider that just one more thing in the bizarro-world that is deployment. Yeah, so that's kind of a heavy thing to drop on you in the morning, but I am always taking stock to see how I am doing, and I really feel built for this type of work. I know many others couldn't do it, and that's okay. I don't know how I am going to be able to communicate that to people other than you, and have them "get it." I imagine there will be a level of curiosity and amazement, which isn't altogether a bad thing. There are some curious and amazing things happening out here. It is hard to get others to see it all in context though. I see how these people have grown accustomed to war and death as a way of life, it happens all too easily and the senses become dull to it. I can at least look at myself and know when I need to step back and search for what might be the "normal" response to some of these instances. Maybe there isn't one, or maybe there is just the socially acceptable and rational response, which is obviously going to be different than what one can feel in theatre. I mean it wasn't thirty minutes after we pronounced him dead, cleaned up all the blood from the floor and had him in a body bag on the stretcher that we were looking at each other and asking each other if we were ready for chow. Odd. But Grey's Anatomy *totally makes more sense to me now.*

So anyways, I was listening to Cold Play this morning in the room and there was a song that I only remember hearing on Grey's, *like when Meredith does her little monologue at the end, and it totally made me miss you. I forget between seasons just how close you and I have gotten watching our little shows each year, and how much our hearts feel as we watch them. I honestly couldn't believe that that little song made me miss you more than the pictures that are on my wall. I guess we were right about shared experiences after all, huh?*

~Matt

I wasn't really sure what to think about Matt describing experiences like these as a "slow day." He found true fulfillment serving the medical personnel in the aid station. I was proud of what he was capable of doing in the moment and grateful he had the support of close friends who were going through it with him.

Only days after this message, around the first of October 2009, I drove out to visit my grandparents in Nebraska. We were concerned that my grandmother was near death, and so my dad and brother were also headed there.

Matt had been trying hard to catch a helicopter ride to visit soldiers at COP Keating. Keating was scheduled to be closed, with the last of our soldiers flying out on October 10th. Keating was about the size of a football field with steep mountains completely surrounding the COP on all sides. The soldiers there, the Black Knight troop, had frequent skirmishes with the Taliban in the surrounding mountains. The helicopter rides had been confined to bringing ammo and supplies. The soldiers had complained of a lack of warm meals and packages from home, and of watching their mail and supplies air-dropped by mistake into the nearby river.

In his last phone call with me before I left for Nebraska, Matt said he was headed to talk with the commander to convince him to put Matt on the next bird to Keating.

I didn't hear from Matt while we were in Nebraska, but that was normal when he was out visiting troops. My brother Shane and his son decided to ride back with me and the boys to visit Colorado and fly back home from there. I appreciated having an extra adult around for a few days.

Shortly after we arrived home, I learned that COP Keating had been attacked by an insurgence of as many as 400 Taliban fighters. Most of the fifty-two American soldiers at Keating had been trained for small groups of twelve, but weren't expecting this. The battle was brutal and lengthy. Fortunately, the commander had not allowed Matt to go to Keating. Instead, Matt watched the horrific battle unfold from the Bostick TOC. I imagined him looking at computer screens on the walls of the TOC, feeling helpless as we lost seven soldiers on the battlefield, another twenty-seven were wounded. Matt's role, again, was with the wounded and dying.

Specialist Stephan Mace was one of the soldiers wounded in the Keating battle. His comrades and medics managed to keep him alive until he could be brought back to Bostick where Zagol, Matt, and the rest of the surgical team and nurses rushed him into surgery. Before Mace went under anesthesia, Matt tried to comfort him by promising to have a beer with him when they got home. He had often told me how he noticed that a person's will to live is harder to maintain once they are under anesthesia.

Despite exhaustive efforts by Zagol and the surgical team, Mace died on the table. Matt wrapped Mace's Saint Christopher medal around his right hand and gave him the Catholic Prayer of Absolution with the help of his Catholic chaplain mentor on the phone from J-bad.

The total now for Keating was eight killed in action, and the wounded were still coming in.

October 4, 2009—Afghanistan

> *Hey Love,*
> *For some reason, the line on my phone keeps ringing busy, so I am not able to call, but I wanted you to know I am back safe on Bostick. Tonight we have the remaining twelve*

"walking wounded" from Keating coming in, so it looks like another long night. I am already pretty exhausted, but this will definitely knock it out of me by tomorrow. The ramp ceremony was not too difficult to get through; it was very sobering to see eight flag-draped caskets laying before me in the belly of that C-17.

By now, the news of what happened here is spreading like wildfire. I even joked with some of the guys in the hospital about who is going to play them in the movie. Only a handful of us will ever know how terrifying yesterday's events were. The world will sensationalize it and make it a rallying point of some sort or another. The killed and wounded will become numbers for one side or the other. But for me, they are my friends, and they have seen hell.

I love you all, go enjoy the day and kiss those boys for me. And send pictures.

All of Me,
Matthew

By the time I heard Matt's voice again, he had counseled most of the Black Knight soldiers, allowing them to recount the horrors of their experience. Matt was so tired he could barely speak. It sounded like he wanted to cry. Maybe he did but didn't let me know it. This was a short call, but the sweetest call I ever had from him. He told me that when it was happening, there was nothing for him to do but wait for the dead and wounded to come in. At the time, they were unsure of what the numbers would be, so he created a makeshift morgue at Bostick.

Over the next several days, Matt continued to debrief with the Black Knight soldiers and performed a memorial ceremony for the fallen. The ceremony made it possible for the soldiers in the unit to pay their respects and say goodbyes, but Matt's job was far from over.

October 9, 2009, 4:34 p.m.—Afghanistan

So, I am finally done with the platoon debriefings and it is a good feeling. I have spent the last few days empathizing with those who felt sheer terror for an extended period of time and I can't say that I have come away unchanged.

I remember years ago, in considering the chaplaincy that Psalm 23 kept coming to mind, especially the part

about walking through the valley of the shadow of death. I just never thought I would see that. I wonder what life is going to look like from this point forward. I wonder how much more I will enjoy you and the boys and the beach next year!
    All my Love,
    Matthew

The soldiers from Keating lost everything, and Matt sent me a list of items they needed. The story was widely covered in the news and many people in America wanted to help and sent boxes of toiletries, food, and even DVD players and video game equipment to replace what was lost. Matt created a "Free-X" where any soldiers could come by and get whatever they needed. Everyone involved was overwhelmed by the kindness from people all over, including the local American Legion, Patriot Riders, churches, and families. Even today, I run into people I hadn't met before who say they sent boxes to support Keating.

I was beginning to worry how Matt was holding up. I knew something was changing in him. How could it not? He sent out an update to family:

October 13, 2009—Afghanistan

    By now, if you have been paying attention to the news at all, you have heard of Eight Heroes who gave their life in defense of Combat Outpost Keating in Kamdesh, Afghanistan on 3 October 2009. What you may not know is that those men were a part of the 3rd Squadron, 61st Cavalry Regiment, my unit.

    Having heard the story of that day from the survivors of the battle, in the critical incident stress debriefs that we conducted when they arrived back to FOB Bostick, it is in no way an overstatement to say that those men gave their lives to save the lives of their brothers on the ground. A group of fifty-two soldiers fought off an onslaught of over 400 insurgents who held the high ground all around, and managed to get inside the wire of the COP. With the help of close-air support helicopters, fixed-wing fast-movers and a B1 bomber, the men of Black Knight troop retook the ground of the COP and obliged 150+ insurgents seeking martyrdom. I had visited my soldiers out at Keating three times before this incident happened, so as they described the details of the battle, I could understand how terrifying it was for them to look up into the mountains all around them, watching a driving rain of bullets and RPGs impact within feet of them as they raced around, attempting to defend themselves and recover the remains of their fallen brothers. The word "Hero" was invented for men such as this . . .

Forevermore, I know what the valley of the shadow of death looks like, and I have looked into the eyes of dozens of men who have walked through it, none unscathed. But know that even in the wake of this event, at a Warrior's Huddle bonfire which we held the night of the memorial, we had three soldiers re-enlist to continue serving for many years to come. We remain steadfast and inspired. And it is good to be around my boys again.

~Matt

After Keating, Matt's duties in Afghanistan kept him well acquainted with death. Over time, some of these experiences started to weigh on him. It brought him a sense of purpose, but was beginning to exhaust him, too. Here is some of our conversation:

November 10, 2009—Afghanistan

The past few days have been spent mired in the muck of moon-dust mud. There is no mud thicker and gooier than that created with powder-fine dirt. The rub of it all is that there can only be two states of such dirt, and both are cumbersome, each in their own right. With one, each breath you breathe is clouded with a mist of finely particulated objects, and with the other, each step you take is an exercise in the futility of attempting to keep the sides of your shoes from becoming caked with sludge. And there is really no way of going about one's life in such an area without going outside several times each hour or simply remaining outside. It is a fascinating existence. And I must admit that for the past few days, my gaze has been ever-downward, focused on the next step, barely taking a moment to scan out several meters or even look at the horizon for fear of busting one's ass and becoming that much more one with the mire.

So you can imagine how refreshing it was to see blue sky this morning, which afforded me a glimpse of the snow-covered mountains in the distance. And for a moment,

I felt my soul pause. I was not faced downward planning my next step, but still and patient. I may have even caught up with myself, and that is no small feat. Clouds lazily circled around the ridgeline....

And for a moment I had not just left the aid station whispering prayers over the fragile body of a three-year-old boy, whose eyelids I sat and held closed until they stayed shut. Dusty and dirty, with no outward signs of trauma, except the testimony of whichever family member it was that brought him to us after he stepped out in front of a truck. I used only one palm to perform rapid chest compressions, all the while whispering to him to just wake up. I wanted to cry, I wanted to feel, but in a place where death is a way of life one must choose what to allow oneself to feel. I and another cleaned him up, after Doc uttered aloud what each of us had been feeling, and our efforts went from attempting to prolong his short life, to preparing to hand him over to his father who was waiting outside. Lifting his limp body and wrapping him in a blanket, the same way he may have been handed to his mother following his birth.

And I wanted to stand alone on top of that snow-covered mountain.

Immediately following his pronouncement, Doc rushed into the OR to begin surgery on the little girl who had come in only moments earlier from being accidentally shot by her brother. She was stable, under anesthetic and intubated, waiting for her tiny abdomen to be explored for damage. Two children came in today, and one survived. And I am convinced I will never know why.

And I want to be surrounded by the silence of those snowy woods.

I have heard that (Frost's) poem is about suicide, and I disagree. It never will be that for me. For me, it will always be that point in the midst of the blizzard where the beauty, which is normally overlooked, interrupts the chaos and ugliness of the world. And for a moment, everything is calm. There are no cares and worries, and it really is just that simple. And then you shake the reigns, and the sled begins moving again, slowly toward a warm, cozy fire. A gracious blanket and cup of warm coffee. Those woods are a diversion. Maybe those woods represent the immensity and depth of a God who can absorb the complexity of my soul.

Maybe as I look into his profound wisdom, he can swallow up my ignorance.

As I held that little body in my hands, I understood the cry of the father who brought his wounded son to Christ. Admitting the conundrum of his faith and disbelief. There are things I cannot understand, Christ. And only to you can I bring them, asking humbly for you to accept this little offering of faltering faith. It is all I have. Can you do something with it?

There is snow on the mountaintops, and as it calls me to look up, my heart is affirmed that I know from whence cometh my strength. I believe, but help my unbelief.

~Matt

November 10, 2009—Colorado

Matthew,

I have no words. At least not many anyways, and maybe that is what I should have been for you yesterday. I just don't understand, I can't fathom your existence there—and I hate that—exactly what I feared. How will I ever know? How will I ever be what you need for me to be when I haven't been there? But I will give you room, all the room you need to tell me about it, to deal with it when it's time. You are so strong in spirit.

I love you so much.

Corie

January 19, 2010—Afghanistan

As I recount the feelings and events that led us to the present, I wish I could hold you and feel you there. So many thoughts and emotions well up in me as I relive this experience. I remember how hopeful we were when all things should have made us hopeless. We should have drowned in the pools of idealism which we walked upon for so many years, oblivious to consequence, status quo or expectations. The word Serendipity has come to mind more than once in the last month ... Last night on the two-hour flight from BAF [Bagram Airfield] to Bostick, all I could imagine was teaching and fathering our boys when I get home. The next time we get the chance to walk them onto a helicopter, to tell them of the freezing cold nights huddled up against a buddy as we buzzed over the snow-covered mountains, and wait to have to tell them about flying in the middle of the night with the flag-covered remains of Stephan Mace, who I had only two hours prior recited the Last Rites of the Catholic Church over, before holding Doc Zagol as he cried after pronouncing dead the soldier he worked so hard to save.

I want to run with those boys, to throw the football and baseball and jump and laugh. I want to enjoy life. I want to collapse in your arms and hold you in mine, knowing that I have seen the worst of humanity, and promising to protect you from it all. I want to look in your eyes across the table at Panera, believing that no one else in the entire coffee shop is as close as we two.

You are Home, for me. Over the years, wherever you are, is Home to me.

Soon, I am coming Home.
All my love,
Matthew

Emotion floods my heart whenever I reread Matt's words, because I remember his tear-stained face when later told me the stories. The pictures in my mind of the events at Keating were made only a little more accurate by the OR and tents I saw the day before in Erbil. These stories, unshared sacred stories, have been my only glimpses into the dark moments of my love's heart.

Each email or call from Matt conveyed his intermittent good spirits or his exhaustion, and it was March before I saw him in front of me and held him in my arms. He had many more significant moments to go through before he came home, including getting shot at on Christmas while visiting his soldiers. I'm glad he didn't tell me about that until he got home.

Finally, after ten months, in March 2010, it was Matt's turn to come home for two weeks of R&R with us before returning to finish his deployment. The boys were in the bathtub when the call came that he had landed in Dallas and would be at the Colorado airport within three hours. I was nervous, but ready to have him home. I notified our family that he was in the States and grabbed a couple of friends to come take pictures at the airport.

The reunion was emotional. The boys cried. Matt cried. We all cried.

He had taken off his cross patches in the plane so no one would know he was a chaplain. He was so spent, he didn't think he could offer comfort to anyone else. I took him to our son's field day before we came home. I settled the boys upstairs so we could talk.

Matt hadn't even taken off his uniform or had a shower before he began to weep. He had been holding it together while the boys were around. He let out everything he'd held in for months. All I could do was hold him.

Matt's parents were understandably excited that he was home and wanted to hear his voice, but he was not ready to talk. His mom called several times before something in him snapped. He jumped up and angrily answered the phone, blasting his mom. In response to her asking how he was doing, he ranted every gruesome detail, every horrific moment, every painful experience. I dared not intervene.

This was the first time I realized Matt was changed. We were both different. We joined the thousands of other families who could say deployment changed them.

After the call, Matt sat down on the couch and asked, "Am I broken?"

He definitely felt that way. I didn't know what to do. Like so many other military spouses, I danced around the minefield of his question.

The two weeks at home re-energized Matt, and he was able to finish the deployment strong. He was actually eager to get back to his soldiers.

When Matt came home at the end of his deployment, we had to learn how to communicate again, need each other again, and respect each other's sacred spaces. We each had experiences we didn't know how to talk about in a way the other could grasp, so we left them alone. One thing we did agree on: we would bring purpose out of what we had each gone through. Matt did his best to be an example for his soldiers on how to manage his life in a way that honored our marriage and family.

Matt was also different physiologically, and he was unhappy with the changes he saw in himself. After a long season of constant performance, Matt was not able to handle stress the way he had before. He felt tired most of the time. His body needed time to recover. Medical evaluations and lab work revealed that his adrenal gland was depleted, probably by repeated adrenaline spikes over the year-long deployment. Adrenal supplements, yoga, and acupuncture helped him recover over time from the aftereffects of managing constant crisis.

Sleep was an issue. Matt had some nightmares, but more often, he simply couldn't turn off his brain to rest. Valium became a regular necessity. Though I never saw behaviors that indicated substance abuse, I didn't like watching him depend on medication to sleep.

His grief over Tyler and others was the first real loss we processed as a couple. I felt the loss and grieved for the families, but Matt and I did not experience that loss in the same way or to the same degree. I had never experienced such loss. Even my grandparents were still living at the time. Matt was going through something I couldn't share, and I did not know how to handle it. He was not the husband I knew before.

A couple of years later, he told me that he talked to Tyler on occasion after his death. Neither of us believed in ghosts or that souls stick around after people die, so I asked him about it and I loved his explanation. Matt said he knew that Tyler might not be able to hear him, but it helped Matt just to talk. He explained that when a person is alive in one place, the only way to reach him is to call him or go to that place where he is. In death, Matt felt Tyler was released from those constraints, so now Matt could talk to Tyler whenever he wanted. It didn't matter if Tyler could hear him or not—that was up to God, not Matt. For him, it was a way to connect.

I better understood what Matt meant when my grandfather died a couple of years later. I had dreaded his death for so long, thinking I wouldn't be able to live through the pain of that loss. But I could celebrate the connection I had with my grandfather whenever the tears came. I didn't have to be afraid of the pain.

Matt still has moments that send him back to Afghanistan. Sometimes he doesn't tell me about them. Other times, our whole day adjusts to whatever he needs to do to stay calm and centered. Every now and then, he still asks, "Do you think I am broken?"

To which I now reply with certainty, "No, you aren't."

For all these reasons, I wanted to see the mountains of Afghanistan, as if I had questions only they could resolve. Most of those questions began with "Why?"

I couldn't say I regretted our experiences, because we loved the community and the bonds we forged in that crucible. But I still carried a grievance. I needed *these* mountains to listen, even though I didn't know how to form my words yet.

Before security was an issue for military families, there was a bumper sticker that said, "Half my heart is in Afghanistan." For me that was true. Half my heart went to Afghanistan, and some of it was stolen and didn't return. Now I had something to leave there, too.

WHERE THE PEBBLE FELL

As the plane wheels hit the runway at Bagram Airfield, I realized how unlikely it was that the loved ones of Tyler Parten or Stephan Mace, or any of the other lost soldiers, would ever see the mountains where their soldiers left this earth. A lump formed in my throat as I felt a weight of my responsibility, and tears threatened to overtake me. I hoped I could do this. I realized I had left my grandfather's handkerchief behind at the hotel when I downsized to the smaller backpack. I was on my own. I took some deep breaths and decided I wouldn't talk to anyone unless I had to. This lump in my throat had a mission of its own.

An F-16 screamed down the runway as we came off the C-17. I took out my camera just in time to capture the second F-16 on video. I hoped to take more videos that day to provide a more panoramic view of the location for those back in the States who were following my journey. Pictures capture a fraction of a second, but videos offer a more complete package of both sight and sound. The mountains demanded my attention. They looked as high as Pikes Peak looked from our home in Colorado, but I knew these mountains were much farther away. I thought, *They must be massive to look so huge from this distance.*

Completely surrounding Bagram, these mountains did not evoke the friendly relationship I shared with the Colorado mountains. Like the witches of Oz, they had different motives. I didn't have much time to think about this before it was time to board a C-130 aircraft for the last leg, to Forward Operating Base Fenty.

I made a video of the moment, speaking into the camera as I walked toward the waiting plane: "We just landed in

Afghanistan. Matt said the mountains were pretty big, and they are much bigger than the mountains in Colorado Springs, that's for sure. I'm pretty tired, I'm exhausted. I think I had about two-and-a-half hours' sleep last night, which is pretty fitting, considering a lot of Matt's time here in Afghanistan was some of the most tiring seasons working with his soldiers. About to get on a C-130. This is pretty remarkable. I'm trying not to cry." I cut the camera off before the lump in my throat won over.

The soldiers on the tarmac were in full kit with weapons, ensuring extra security for the secretary of defense. This was very different from seeing soldiers on TV in all their gear. I tried not to imagine each one patrolling a dangerous mountainside. All I could see was Tyler in full gear hiking into the mountains. I needed to re-capture my thoughts.

The propellers were spinning and the wind was strong. We had to push hard to move forward to board from the back of the plane. The inside of the plane was divided into halves. Two rows of canvas seats faced each other along each half. The two middle rows were back to back. The press sat on the right half of the plane, and the secretary and his staff were on the left. I chose a seat and buckled in.

Like the C-17, all the wires, tubes, and parts were exposed, giving it an industrial feel, and it had the same musty diesel smell of other Air Force planes. I don't think aesthetics are part of the interior design of a military cargo plane. Once again, there were few windows, and I felt momentarily disappointed that I wouldn't see more of Bagram, knowing it was a significant place for many military families.

We took off quickly in more ways than one. The C-130 accelerated faster than any plane I'd been on before and went into a steep climb as soon as we lifted off. My emotion subsided and was replaced with euphoria. I was taken by the impressive flight maneuvers. For a moment as the plane banked sharply to the right, I could look across the aisle to the window and look straight down on the snowcapped and rugged mountains. There were so many of them, not a ridge line or a row of peaks—a seemingly never-ending landscape of mountains after mountains. I thought about cavalry scouts trying to find

Taliban leaders in this territory of endless peaks and was immediately discouraged.

As I looked at the mountains, I wanted to begin my argument with them, but I was still trying to hold it together in front of everyone. So I stared at the mountains and thought of how much had been sacrificed in this territory. Many had lost their innocence, and some lost their lives.

The flight was only thirty minutes, and the landing was just as fast as the take off—with a sharp decline and an abrupt stop, as if they anticipated a short runway and someone shooting the plane on the way in. If this was the combat flight of a C-130 Matt told me about, I could totally see why he loved it.

We walked down the ramp of the plane and saw a group of buildings surrounded by waist-high cement barricades. The installation appeared small compared to Bagram and Baghdad. This was FOB Fenty.

To my surprise and confusion, the first thing I saw were the memorials I'd seen in pictures Matt showed me of Jalalabad. Were we at Fenty or Jalalabad? The answer was both. FOB Fenty is the forward operating base in the city of Jalalabad. Here was another example of not fully understanding locations Matt told me about. I had misunderstood even some of the basic information my soldier told me. I wondered how frustrating that must have been for him. Did he think I didn't care enough to listen or to remember what he said? This was more than a place on our itinerary for the day. This was a place my husband had actually been!

The memorial plaques on the stone walls at the entrance to the base honored units that had served there and listed the names of fallen troops. The 4th Infantry Division was one of those units. During my visit, the 10th Mountain Division was stationed there.

While Matt was based at FOB Bostick, the leadership for 4th Brigade Combat Team was at FOB Fenty. I immediately thought of our brigade commander Colonel Randy George. His wife Patty, also a West Point graduate, was a firecracker, always planning events to pull the families together at home. Patty started a running group for the spouses, as well as a "Climb to Afghanistan" program, in which spouses tracked the miles they walked during the deployment with the goal of reaching the number of miles from Colorado to Afghanistan. She was the originator of the 4th Brigade t-shirt, which I took with me when I traveled those miles myself.

Our brigade chaplain, Father Paul Madej, who mentored Matt, had been stationed at FOB Fenty during Matt's deployment. From Fenty, the brigade leaders handled extremely challenging situations and historic battles. This was home base for the injured and those needing respite. I knew without a doubt our leaders cared about our soldiers and their families during the deployment. Of the fifty-four losses in the brigade during that deployment, eleven were from our squadron, 3-61CAV. The months of late 2009 and early 2010 changed the lives of thousands of military families, as they experienced the ongoing stress, injuries, and deaths of their soldiers.

I was given a moment with Secretary Carter just before we entered Fenty. I'd been holding back my emotions in order to get through this moment, and I couldn't think of words to convey what I was feeling. I did my best to relay to him that this place was close to the location where Matt had been deployed.

"Thank you so much for bringing me here," I managed to say through my tears. "We lost so many."

I don't regret not saying more. There's no way to convey a deeply personal narrative within the time it takes to greet someone with a handshake. Our military story is like hundreds, if not thousands, Secretary Carter had heard before.

Other than when he welcomed me on the first leg of the journey, this was my only chance to interact with the secretary. He and his wife, Stephanie, and I took a few pictures together, and the moment was over. The rest of the press had been taken to the USO, and I walked with the staff members following the secretary. We passed between the two stone walls with several memorial plaques on each side. On one of the plaques, I noted the distinctive quartet of ivy leaves that adorns the 4th Infantry Division symbol.

My mind flooded with memories from Colorado. During the months before Matt's first deployment, he encouraged me to attend a predeployment training for spouses for the "care team." He said the care team would be a good fit for my skills as a counselor and a good way to be involved. I quickly learned that military spouses volunteer a lot, whether out of kindness, getting out of the house, or maintaining a resumé. My boys were young then, only five and two. I had just shut down my private practice in Georgia to follow our new calling into the military world, so volunteering seemed like a good solution.

Matt was right. Care team was right up my alley or, as the military likes to say, "in my lane." In the training, I learned the military protocol for when a service member is wounded or killed in action. Not many spouses signed up for this training, because few spouses want to focus on the worst-case scenario, especially right before a deployment. In addition to instruction about how the military notifies family members of casualties, care team training covered the stages of grief and how to talk with and support bereaved family members. I had learned much of this information in my training to be a counselor, but now it was personal. I worked hard to keep my own anxiety down, reminding myself that Matt was going to a relatively safe place.

In the days closer to the deployment, the squadron recognized the need for a care team coordinator to connect the various teams of spouses who would respond and support families after a death or injury. Although I didn't claim to be an expert on grief, I felt I could do the job and agreed to do it for 3-61CAV. My responsibilities included serving on the "Go-Team" for our squadron. This meant I would join the commander's wife and the rear-detachment commander to follow up with families in our squadron who received a death notification.

This was where I first learned the protocols following when a soldier was killed in action—the blackout of the whole squadron with all communication cut off. Soldiers in Class A uniforms then notified affected families in person—the "knock on the door" no family wants to receive. After the official notification, the Go-Team waited close by in case the spouse or family wanted company and support.

Captain Corey Steiner, our rear detachment commander at the time, was responsible for caring for families back home during the deployment. Rear detachment is a tough, often thankless, job. While he handled the military logistics that were in his job description, Captain Steiner also served as point person for hundreds of military spouses. His responsibilities often kept him away from home, requiring much sacrifice from his wife as well.

My task as a coordinator seemed simple enough. I could call upon spouse volunteers to provide hot meals and other support after the Go Team made initial contact. With two little boys at home, one in the midst of potty training, I didn't have a lot of time on my hands, but I thought I could manage it. How bad could it be?

The Go-Team was deployed for the first time when Jason Fabrizi was killed. A task I thought would take a couple of hours took all day as we tried to locate his wife. I didn't mind waiting, but I felt sick to my stomach through most of it. All I could think of was wherever Jason's wife was, she was enjoying her last few moments of normal life, even if it was grocery shopping. I could have waited forever.

Eventually, it was time. The green suits notified her, giving her only the details they were allowed to provide. Susan Brown, the 3-61CAV commander's wife, and I went in to sit with her. I remember walking up the Fabrizis' sidewalk and seeing the Blue Star flag flying in the window. I was still so new to military life, I had to ask Susan what it meant. She sighed and told me it meant a soldier was deployed. I never saw that flag the same way again and refuse to have one myself.

While Matt was performing the memorial service in Afghanistan and counseling his soldiers, this job was one way I could be an extension of him at home. It made me feel like we were still a team, serving together with a common mission. I came home that day emotionally spent.

Sometimes spouses came to me if they were concerned about their soldier. I let Matt know about their concerns, with their permission, so he could check on the soldiers to put spouses' minds at ease. Soldiers knew they didn't have to be in dire need to come to the chaplain. He was available for everyday concerns, and could perhaps head off some issues before they ballooned. This was one way couples got the help and connection they needed.

As the care team coordinator, I was notified early on in a

blackout in case my assistance was needed for the Go-Team. When Tyler Parten was killed, Matt had called just before the blackout to ask me to keep an eye on Tyler's girlfriend. The formal notification was made first to his mother.

When the soldiers who fought with Tyler on the mountainside came home to recover from their wounds, I went to the hospital. I wanted to provide them with an extension of the support they had from Matt in theater.

Once a month, Fort Carson held a memorial service in honor of soldiers from the installation who died. During Tyler's exceptionally difficult ceremony, I visualized Matt providing a similar one on the other side of the world.

When the Keating battle took place in 2009, I had just returned from Nebraska with my brother, Shane. I was awakened at 5:30 a.m. by a call from Captain Steiner.

"Your husband is all right," were the first words he spoke. Then he asked me to come into the office. We were already in blackout.

I asked Shane to watch the boys for the day, telling him I had no idea when I'd be back. The timeliness of my brother's visit was an act of God that still moves me to tears. While I was at the Rear Detachment Office, an email came from Matt, which he sent just before the blackout took effect.

October 3, 2009, 9:46 a.m.—Afghanistan

> *Hey Love,*
> *I can't call you right now. It may be a good thing if your brother could stay for a few days longer than maybe he expected to, in order to help with the boys. You have the potential to be needed a lot in the next three to four days. Tell him to consider it service to the country. I love you, I love you, I love you. Do not say anything to anyone about this. Do not allude to anything with your brother. Just ask him to stay for a little while longer. Please let me know when Corey calls you.*
> *All my love,*
> *Matthew*

Corey Steiner's office was swarming with soldiers, or maybe I was moving in slow motion. I sat in front of his desk as he explained that Keating was under attack. I remembered that last phone call from Matt, when he said he was going to make every effort to reach Keating. Even while Captain Steiner assured me that Matt was at FOB Bostick, I panicked on the inside. *Is he at Keating? He doesn't carry a weapon!* As noncombatants, chaplains don't carry weapons. An enlisted soldier, a chaplain assistant, carries a weapon to provide protection when needed so the chaplain can carry out his duties caring for the wounded and dying. I couldn't help but create images and scenarios in my mind: *Is Matt trapped there? Where is he?*

As I finally accepted, Matt was indeed at Bostick, safe from at least one kind of harm.

Captain Steiner said he knew the unit had at least one missing, and the biggest concern was whether the enemy had taken him. Soldiers continued to run in and out of the captain's office with updates. There were five confirmed killed in action, but notification of families could not begin until that battle was over. Captain Steiner had a white board in his office, where names were listed in three columns, "KIA," "MIA," or "Unknown."

I was afraid names would just keep coming. I was trying to understand what was happening and wished I had paid more attention to the maps Matt had shown me of the theater of operations.

"How bad is this?" I asked Captain Steiner.

"This is really bad," was all he said.

We knew we had more than three families in the local area to notify and realized our three-member Go-Team wasn't enough. Captain Steiner had to remain in his office to manage the flow of information. Susan and I needed to split up. We called in Patty George, the brigade commander's wife, to help. She had already played a big part in preparing for the deployment, and the families were familiar with her. Both Patty's and Susan's husbands were also deployed and under an immense amount of pressure to coordinate efforts to help our guys at Keating.

When the battle was over, with eight of our soldiers confirmed killed in action, the number of wounded was still unknown, but the Casualty Assistance Office could at least begin death notifications. The Go-Team followed in the wake of the sad news. The plan was for each of us to visit one family alone, then check back in with Captain Steiner for the next name and address in need of our care. This was a nightmare.

The first name I received was Amanda.

I pulled up and stopped a few doors down from her house. She had already been notified. I called Captain Steiner to let him know I found her address. He confirmed she was willing to have someone from the unit visit her.

I knocked. When Amanda opened the door, her eyes were red, her tears still flowing.

"I'm Chaplain Weathers' wife," I said. "Justin was one of his soldiers."

I sat with her at a table in the front room. I don't remember what the house looked like or even what kind of table it was. I just remember Amanda, a beautiful woman with blonde hair pulled up in a ponytail. Her soldier was Sergeant Justin Gallegos. They had recently divorced, but they were still close. They had a beautiful son. Justin had arranged for Amanda to watch over his truck and other belongings while he was deployed. More importantly, he had designated her as the next of kin to be notified if anything happened to him. Amanda was also an active duty soldier, a medic.

She asked me questions about what was happening at Keating, but I didn't have many answers. I had been trained to not provide additional details outside of what the notification team already told her. I was devastated for her and allowed my own tears to fall. She was frustrated that more information wasn't available, but as a soldier herself she knew the protocol. Someone from the back room brought a baby girl out to her. My heart dropped. She also had a daughter.

Amanda pieced together a few facts and figured out that the battle had been a big one and that there might be other casualties. Slightly breaking the rules I learned in training, I acknowledged that was possible. Here was a woman in front of me whose world was crumbling. Staying strictly and coldly on protocol didn't make human sense. None of this made sense. I stayed with her for three hours. When I left, I thanked her for letting me sit with her and gave her my number for anything she might need, anytime. I told her we would coordinate with other spouses to provide meals and anything else she needed. We hugged and said goodbye for now.

I cried all the way back to my car. I was overwhelmed and needed to prepare to knock on the next front door. I felt guilty that my soldier was still alive while others were not, and I wondered about my soldier. *How was Matt? What was he doing?*

I called Steiner from my car to tell him I was ready for the next house.

I didn't get home until evening. Shane had done an amazing job with the boys. He was taken aback by this glimpse into another world, seeing the human cost of military losses.

My neighbor, whose husband was in Iraq, heard something had happened in Afghanistan where Matt was stationed and came to check on me. I opened the door, told her Matt was fine, and then I cried. Without asking any questions, she brought her kids, ages nine, ten, and twelve over to my house, and together that family completely cleaned my house. I had never known kindness quite like that, but I was still new to military life then.

We took several days to locate and notify all the families, so the communications blackout could end. Those days were a blur. I'm not sure when I finally spoke with Matt.

Meanwhile, the press wanted more information. As the care team coordinator, and because my spouse was at the affected location, I was asked to speak at a press conference to address the well-being of the families. The public affairs office spent two days preparing and training me for the press conference. We role-played scenarios in which the press might try to get more information from me than I could give. I kept wondering why anyone would do that. I was exhausted and only pushed through because of all the support around me. Matt sent a message for me to include in my remarks.

Fort Carson Coping With Tragic Day In Afghanistan
AP/DAN ELLIOTT
    FORT CARSON, Colo., Oct. 7, 2009—The Pentagon announcement Wednesday confirmed their worst fears—the eight American soldiers killed in a bloody weekend attack

in Afghanistan were all from a single Fort Carson unit. But commanders here insisted that the unit's morale is rebounding.

"They were attacked, the unit fought bravely, and in the end, they won the day," said Maj. Daniel Chandler, the rear detachment commander for the 4th Brigade Combat Team, 4th Infantry Division. "The brave soldiers that we lost and all of the comrades that were left there, there were a lot of heroes on that day," he said.

Hundreds of insurgents armed with automatic rifles and rocket-propelled grenades attacked the soldiers at two US outposts in Nuristan province Saturday, causing one of the highest US death tolls in Afghanistan in a single battle in more than a year.

The Defense Department had already said that at least some of the eight soldiers killed were from the Colorado Springs-area base.

Wednesday's announcement that all were from a Fort Carson brigade that has seen some of the fiercest fighting in Iraq and Afghanistan came with their names: Staff Sgt. Vernon W. Martin, 25 of Savannah, Ga.; Sgt. Justin T. Gallegos, 27, of Tucson, Ariz.; Sgt. Joshua M. Hardt, 24, of Applegate, Calif.; Sgt. Joshua J. Kirk, 30, of South Portland, Maine; Spc. Michael P. Scusa, 22, of Villas, N.J.; Spc. Christopher T. Griffin, 24, of Kincheloe, Mich.; Spc. Stephan L. Mace, 21, of Lovettsville, Va.; and Pfc. Kevin C. Thomson, 22, of Reno, Nev.

Fort Carson commanders offered their condolences to the soldiers' families and said that support teams have contacted them. The commanders also said that the families of four of the victims were living in Colorado Springs at the time of the deaths but officials weren't sure if they were still in Colorado.

Corie Weathers, whose husband, Matt, is a chaplain in Afghanistan with the brigade, said her husband has told her that since the battle, "They have had moments of laughter to the point of tears in the midst of their grieving."

Weathers said her husband told her: "We are taking a moment to pause and hug each other over the loss of our brothers. However, we will be ready for the next mission at hand."

The care teams, although they had been well prepared, were not ready for this kind of mass casualty event. All the bereaved families who lived in the area were in need of meals. Patty asked the entire brigade to step up to help. Within the day we had three freezers stocked with meals for families. The biggest challenges came in unexpected ways.

Amanda called and said she was doing as well as could be expected, but found her greatest needs were during evening hours when she was trying to feed her kids and get them to bed. It was taking everything she had to get through each evening.

I called through my list of potential volunteers, but most had deployed husbands and had children of their own. I called more women outside our brigade on the installation and still couldn't find help. By this point, my brother had left; I had tapped out my neighbors, and frankly, had already spent too much time away from my own children. I felt incredible guilt for not stepping in to help more, but was physically unable to do so. As I dialed Amanda's number, I didn't know how to tell her I couldn't help her or find other help. Surprisingly, she was doing better and said that pushing through the evening might actually help her. I wrote this during that week:

Friday, October 9, 2009—Colorado/Corie's Journal

> *So much has changed. All I know is that it's been a rough, but beautiful week. I have been on the phone more than I have wanted to, but wouldn't have traded one discussion I had with these families. I have sat and held someone as they cried. I have encouraged and assured them that there is no right way to grieve, only positive ways to move forward each moment. I have seen God move in my own life as I attempted to connect with others who needed Him through me. I have felt Him calm my fears and hold back sickness like a dam holding a river. I have seen Him make twenty people or more completely unavailable so He could move in someone's life without others there. I have seen my community of friends reach out to offer me anything I needed. I have seen good people have compassion, what a joy it is to see people love others. What sweet healing comes from listening to someone tell their story and feel*

their tension release. What an honor it is to be someone they feel safe around.

I wish I had answers. I wish I understood evil, death, and life's consequences from bad decisions. I wish I had power beyond even God's to deliver to their soul the love He has for them and break down the lies that sweep in. But even though I am tired, sometimes feeling I have no words left, I wouldn't trade where I am—where Matt is—for anything.

Someone asked me if I fear where Matt is now, if my anxiety is different now that I have seen the outposts breached that he regularly visits. My answer was yes. I do feel fear and at any point my mind can think terrible things, but the truth is in the peace I have had since we drove onto this post. I know he is where he should be, I know that God needed him there, and me here. I was brought to tears when driving back on post from the grocery store yesterday. There was an older gentleman bundled up in the cold outside our gate holding a sign that simply said, "Thank you."

I guess I can say "You're welcome" now, and that feels really good to know that he gets it.

Tensions were rising within the family members at home as their grief turned to righteous anger. They wanted to know why their soldiers were at Keating when it was scheduled to be shut down. The soldiers who survived the battle lost everything and left Keating with only what they had on them. Keating had been destroyed, which meant the families who had lost their soldiers would never receive their loved ones' personal effects. None were left.

The stress of so many tasks and emotions caused a momentary disagreement between Susan and me, mostly because we were both trying to do our best to serve the families and couldn't keep track of who was doing what. One day I took my care team binder into Captain Steiner's office, slammed it on the desk in frustration, and said, "I'm done."

He knew I wasn't really done. We were all just very tired, yet we still had a long way to go. We talked. I calmed down and picked up my binder again. As a team, we continued to do our best, doing what we were able to do for the families, while balancing what we could not do. There was just no way to give them what they really wanted and needed—their soldiers back.

When I arrived at FOB Fenty, I was imagining the faces of those families. I felt the weight of their grief and loss and my own husband's losses mixed with my exhaustion. I wanted the families of the fallen to be there with me, to have the closure of being in that place. At Fenty, I relived those days of intense sorrow as if the location carried a newsreel of memories from all who had passed through there.

The secretary of defense was meeting privately with the 10th Mountain Division command, now in charge of that region of Afghanistan. The press was still at the USO. The rest of the secretary's staff and I were taken to a holding room in the building to wait. It was a basic building with mostly bare walls except for a few safety and awareness posters.

I started looking for a restroom so I could give the lump in my throat the freedom to take over in private. I wandered down a hall, but only found a short scraggly Christmas tree, apparently chopped down somewhere nearby, with a single bag of candy canes underneath. There were security personnel in the hallway, as well as extra soldiers waiting for someone outranking them to tell them what to do next. I didn't want to wander too far, afraid of getting lost, left behind, or scolded by security. In short, there was nowhere to go for a good cry.

As I sat in the holding room with Johnny Michael, Major Brindle, and the secretary's speechwriter, my tears finally refused to stay down. I couldn't hide it for long. It was the kind of stifled ugly cry that finally forced me to gasp for air. All eyes turned to me. Major Brindle approached me and asked if there was anything he could do.

I managed to say, "We lost a lot of people close by to here, and I'm a little overwhelmed." I really didn't care if he actually understood. I didn't feel it was necessary to make anyone understand. I didn't expect anyone there to understand my connection to this place.

Johnny came up, leaned over, and wryly said, "Allergies, huh?"

I looked up and smiled. I appreciated the humor to break the tension.

I finally understood a small piece of what combat veterans

feel—the feeling of being connected to an event so intense and utterly life-changing, while surrounded by people who don't understand. When Matt came home for R&R, he felt not only misunderstood, but broken somehow. Broken because his memories brought tears and because of a connection he had to a place and an event that no one around him understood. No matter how much he talked about it, how much he described it, the listener could *not* understand unless he or she had been *through* it. He was hurt by the way people looked at him when he tried to explain, or when he didn't.

I saw that look in the eyes of people around me, an uncomfortable look that said, "I want to help, but I don't know what to do with this."

Even though their intent was kind, the uncertainty in their eyes revealed the distance between us. They had not walked through that valley.

For me, those who understood were in the sisterhood of the 3-61CAV spouses who bonded through the blackouts, served hot meals to our sisters whose lives were changed forever, and vowed to be family when our households felt fractured. Those who had stepped in and held me up are the ones who share that memory with me, like Zagol and Matt's other buddies did for him during and after the tragedy at Keating.

What I needed in that moment in the waiting room was the okay to express my emotions when they spilled out. I needed those who didn't understand to admit they couldn't and still give me permission to feel something. The men sitting in that room did that for me on one level, but I still felt a certain amount of shame for my vivid uncontrollable reaction.

I felt embarrassed.

Then I didn't care.

I wondered if they were afraid I was going to lose it.

Then I thought, *They need to see what is happening to me.*

They needed to see inside the heart and emotions of a military spouse who just landed in the place where her husband changed, where her marriage and her life changed.

We listen to our soldiers recount trauma and combat. We see them come home different. We see our friends' spouses come home different. We sit with families who ache to be where it all ended for their husband, wife, son, or daughter.

You wanted to bring a spouse here? Well, this is what happens when you bring her to where shit got real and her life changed, too.

I may not have touched a dead body, but death had a ripple effect in my life and in our community, and I was standing as close as I would ever get to where the pebble fell.

ROLE REVERSAL

The USO strengthens America's military service members by keeping them connected to family, home and country, throughout their service to the nation.
~USO Mission Statement

I managed to regain my composure that day as we found our way to the USO. Fenty was definitely small and remote compared to Bagram or Baghdad, the main airbases in and out of Afghanistan and Iraq. But some of the locations where Matt and others served were deep in the mountains. After hearing about Keating's inability to get packages from home for months at a time, I was a bit surprised to see a USO at Fenty.

I was even more surprised to meet Regina Wages, a sweet woman who told me she had lived there for more than five years, working every day at the USO. Who would give up so much of her life to serve troops out here in Afghanistan? I believe I asked that out loud, because she explained she had worked in a police department previously and couldn't picture her life any other way. She loved these soldiers, and it made her happy to be here for them. That was apparent as she walked me to the restroom where I could change into my 4th Brigade t-shirt.

The troops we passed lit up when she walked by. She had a maternal camaraderie with them that was apparently earned and respected. I watched as she slapped them on the back, joked, and told them she just made fresh coffee in the USO. I smiled as I took note of the spark in her eye and the lightness in her step that indicated to me Regina was doing what she loved. This time I was not embarrassed when tears welled up in my eyes.

"Thank you for being here," I said to Regina. "I had no idea you were here. Thank you for sacrificing so much."

I couldn't find the right words to tell her what her presence meant to me. A service member is deployed to do a job, and most days it's just a job. But other days, exhaustion, injury, and trauma sweep in, powerful enough to make grown men cry. Yet here is this angel, an adoptive mother with fresh coffee, safe hugs, and help to a phone to call home. Regina's mission is just as much a gift to families at home as it is to the troops she serves directly.

She took in my halting words and hugged me. Handing me her card, she said, "Anything you ever need, honey. You just let me know."

I knew she meant it; the spirit of service came naturally to her. I told her why I was there and asked if she could connect me with some of the troops to talk to them about their experiences.

"Absolutely!" she said and led me back outside to the memorials where a circle of kitted up soldiers were taking a smoke break.

At this point, I was feeling less afraid of doing something wrong and more determined to do what I was there to do. The schedule moved quickly; if I didn't take advantage of moments I had to speak with people, I would miss my window. I love conversations, stories, and encouraging whoever is in front of me. I felt my own spark reigniting. She walked me up to the guys and introduced me.

"I'm a military spouse, and I traveled here to see a little of what life is like during deployment. Can I ask you a few questions about what you feel families don't quite understand?"

The guys were wearing 10th Mountain Division patches on their sleeves, but obviously knew the history of the 4th Infantry Division in the region. They recognized the 4ID ivy insignia.

"You're wearing a 4ID shirt, you can ask whatever the hell you want!" said one.

The guys didn't hold back. They were happy with the conditions there, although many of their family members assumed, as I did, that because they were in Afghanistan they were automatically in harm's way. They pointed to the tall concrete wall in the distance across the tarmac, similar to the ones I had seen in Baghdad.

"As long as we don't go outside those walls, we are really safe here."

While we were talking, helicopters flew along the wall line. I thought that might indicate extra security for the secretary's visit, keeping the enemies on the other side from trying something foolish. Matt used to say "Popshot Johnnies," as they were called, sometimes lobbed a random shot inside the wire just to remind the Americans they were out there.

"I've been here a couple times now," said one cavalry scout. "I used to not be able to talk to my family for three months while I lived somewhere remote in the mountains. Now, I can access the Wi-Fi from the USO building from out here if I want."

Another mentioned that their schedules are often random, and that his family struggles to understand why he is available all day for three days straight, but then on mission for another three days and have no connectivity.

One of the scouts was especially eager to help with my goal of understanding the deployment experience. I told him Matt had been deployed in some remote bases, so the young soldier wanted to show me a B-hut, short for barracks hut, a small one- or two-room building made mostly out of plywood and two-by-fours. B-huts were used at Fenty for various purposes, including sleeping quarters for troops. The ones I saw were built on top of cinder blocks with barbed wire underneath, apparently to keep critters out. A few troops were huddled inside the B-hut we visited, likely trying to avoid the pomp and circumstance of a VIP visit. They all had weapons slung behind their backs. When my guide introduced me and told them why I was there, they all stared as though a unicorn had just walked in.

All were unmarried, but they singled out one poor guy, who apparently had a girlfriend.

"Ask him your questions. He might as well be married."

We left them laughing and walked back toward the memorial where Regina waited for me. The scout who was giving me the guided tour told me this was his fifth deployment. He said he hated it and loved it; he knew it was hard on his family.

The other 10th Mountain soldiers were standing outside the

steps of the USO when we got back there, and one told me he had been at Fenty since September. Trying to do the math in my head, I realized I had forgotten what month we were in. When I had to ask, the guys laughed and pointed to the single strand of tinsel wrapped around the railing of the USO steps.

"It's December!"

Unashamed, I pointed out how minimal the decorations were and how easy it was to forget. They nodded in agreement. Every day feels the same around here, they agreed, Groundhog Day. They said it wasn't bad though and credited the USO with creating events to pass the time and mark the holidays.

"On Thanksgiving we had a Turkey Trot Run where the USO guy dressed up in a turkey costume, and we all had to run after him and catch him," said one guy.

A picture flashed in my mind of Matt's Christmas in Afghanistan when someone dressed up like Santa but kept his weapon on. Soldiers had taken turns sitting on his lap.

Although the FOB had decorations, including an inflatable Santa and airplane complete with twirling propeller, it was apparent that the decor was not what made this place festive.

I asked Regina to take a picture of me in front of the 4th Infantry Division memorial. She insisted on getting her nice camera to document the moment. We went back inside the USO, where the press group was already connected to Wi-Fi to file that day's stories.

I could have logged onto Facebook to connect with everyone back at home, but it didn't feel like the right moment. I missed Matt and the boys terribly, but I wanted to focus on where I was. There was more to take in. I could have spent the whole day looking around and learning.

Everyone was quiet, so I thought it was a good chance for me to make another video. I especially wanted to send a message from Fenty. I found a small room the size of a closet, with *Sesame Street* decals all over the walls. It was used for soldiers to record videos of themselves reading children's books to send home to their kids. Inside was a plush chair, a tripod, and some children's books—a perfect nook for my video. I closed my eyes and allowed myself to step back into the emotional weight of imagining Matt walking through here years ago. I thought about him calling me, exhausted from his own grief and carrying the stories of traumatized soldiers. After losing Tyler, and then after Keating, Matt still had five months to go before he could come home for his two-week R&R.

February, 17, 2010— Afghanistan

It's been a good day, even with as incredibly tired as I am. As Austin Powers would put it, "I am spent." I am tap-dancing in the small puddle at the bottom of a well I have been tapping for energy and compassion. I know it's there and it won't run dry, though.

And so here I am typing away, wishing I could pour the flood of feelings and thoughts out onto paper so that as you all wake up this morning; you know exactly where I am at. I find myself having to distract myself before falling asleep at night sometimes, because I can still see the blank stares of my friends before we processed their remains onto the HLZ for their last flight home. And then I think about how much I want to hold the little hands of my boys, and cry into the nape of my wife's neck like an infant begging for consolation, and what this Independence Day will actually mean for me. And I wouldn't trade any of it, because I am so changed for the better, so alive to the world, so awake to its pain and pleasure. And for the first time in two decades of hearing Dylan's "A Hard Rain's A-Gonna Fall," I understand every word, and term and feeling. And the gospel seems palpably real and pertinent and true and meaningful and necessary. Where hunger is ugly and the souls are forgotten, and I'll tell it, and speak it, and think it and breathe it, and reflect from the mountain so all souls can see, and I'll know my song well before I start singing. And I wonder, when I look my mother and father in the eyes, will they think, "what did you see my blue-eyed son, and where have you been, my darling young one?"

~Matt

Within that five months before Matt's R&R, plenty more stretched him. A soldier of Matt's had a wife, also a soldier and also deployed, but in a different location. She had—against her husband's wishes—decided to ride in a convoy to his location to surprise him. The convoy was hit, and by the time she got to

Doc Zagol's OR, there was nothing they could do, despite an extensive attempt to save her. Matt was there when Doc attempted to stop her from bleeding out. Her husband had been notified that she was in the surgical tent, and he waited in the chapel with his first sergeant. Matt returned to the chapel to notify him that his wife had died, and the soldier was escorted to sit with her remains as they waited on the bird to take them both to Bagram. At the soldier's request, Matt slipped her wedding ring off and handed it to him.

When Matt stepped off the flight coming back from the ramp ceremony at Bagram, he received a Red Cross message for another soldier, ten days away from going home, that his mother, a police officer, had been killed in the line of duty. It was Matt's job to notify the soldier.

I was sitting at a group Bible study when my phone rang with that familiar number: The one caller ID identified as Maryland, but which was never Maryland. I went to a private room and listened to his frail voice over the phone. His mind and body were exhausted.

"I feel like death and I are holding hands and skipping through the daisies," he said. He acknowledged that his job was to "walk through the valley of the shadow of death," but it was happening so much he needed a break.

In his exhaustion, his humor still came through as he tried to cheer himself up, saying that at least he and death were becoming friends considering how much they were "hanging out." I was worried. He needed sleep, but there was nothing I could do, no comfort I could offer, no way I could imagine what he was going through.

Six months after he came home, we sat down to watch *Grey's Anatomy*, just like we did before the deployment. In one scene, the camera angle was from above, looking down on an empty operating table and blood all over the floor. Afterward, I found Matt upstairs, collapsed in the hallway, sitting on the floor, staring at the wall, sobbing.

"What's wrong?" I asked, as I sat next to him. He'd had a flashback of the wife who was killed in the convoy.

"There was so much blood, everywhere, so much blood. We tried to save her," he said with tears in his eyes, still staring at the wall. So many of the deaths he saw were difficult, but losing the wife of a fellow soldier was even harder to take.

I know that when he occasionally asks if I think he is broken, he feels a deep sadness over what evil can make someone do, and the horror of what he saw in war that he can't un-see. As I've worked with other service members in therapy, they are haunted by the image of their buddy's body parts they had to pick up, the smell of burning flesh after a vehicle is hit with an RPG, or the screams of a soldier who couldn't be saved. These are the sights, smells, and sounds the human psyche isn't built to compartmentalize, much less make sense of.

Combat veterans often feel broken when thoughts from the past invade the present, leaving them wanting to curl into fetal positions, when five minutes ago they were fine. My husband isn't broken, not to me and not to our kids. He has experienced life in a more vivid and real way than I ever will. Though I sometimes envy his *carpe diem* outlook, I will never wish to see and experience what he has.

Sitting in Fenty's USO *Sesame Street* recording closet, I allowed myself to feel my own exhaustion and how it must have been for Matt. I allowed myself to feel the fatigue along with the emotions he had carried. Feeling exhausted, thinking back on that time in our lives, knowing he had been somewhere close to where I was sitting, brought back the helplessness I felt when he called me that day claiming to be best buds with death.

Another soldier, a scout from 10th Mountain Division, came up behind me, excited to tell me about the purpose of the recording closet. I had given in to my own flashbacks and allowed myself to become emotional again. When I turned to face him, with tears streaming down my face, he apologized.

"Oh, I'm so sorry," said the scout. "Oh no, did you lose your husband here?"

He had a look that said he didn't know what to do next. For a moment I felt silly. Explaining it to him brought more tears, so I just let it happen, thankful that it wasn't an ugly cry this time. I told him about my project of trying to experience everything I could about deployment. Being here made me feel closer to what Matt went through, perhaps able to understand what I thought I would never understand. It provided a context for where his voice came from when he called.

I could see why the scout thought I was grieving, and I wondered if I sounded crazy.

To my surprise and relief, he lit up. "That's awesome!" he said. "I can't believe they let you do that! What a great idea!"

He had been married twice, and he too had been on several deployments. He looked at me with eyes that understood what deployment must have looked like to us. Anxious to give me his perspective on what family members didn't understand, he talked about his first wife's battle with mental illness. Much of their deployment communication was filled with negativity and unproductive venting that left him feeling helpless. There was so little he could do for her from there, and it was hard on him.

Sometime later, his wife took her own life. I felt silly now for my tears and said so.

He was fascinated that my soldier husband was at home receiving our household goods and setting up for Christmas.

"That's amazing how you switched roles with each other," he said. "It would be interesting to hear what his thoughts are, too."

Looking back on his first marriage, he had learned how important it was for each partner to have his or her own separate support system. Now remarried, he said he and his current wife were doing a much better job. "We talk about the important stuff, and we save the venting and problems for those who are around us who can actually help."

I remarked on how truly important it is to understand the right kind of support for a couple. I didn't regret our decision for me to be Matt's go-to person, though in reality, I'm not sure if I really *was* that person. He had best friends there who became the person I couldn't be. After my first breakdown that morning, I realized how thankful I was for those who were with him when I couldn't be, who supported him and loved him. They served him and made sure he got the rest he needed. I was more grateful than ever now for those relationships and would do everything possible to encourage him to keep them.

With tables turned, I wasn't sure what I would do if Matt were to need me back in the States while I was in Afghanistan. I would feel powerless and unable to finish what I was there to do and yet have no way of getting home. I would be paralyzed.

I was confident Matt would be able to handle whatever came up. This is what gives many successful military couples such a resilient grit. At some point, the one at home has to say, "You can't help me, so I'll figure it out even if I hate the fact that you're gone."

I have been there, and it is tempting to not go to an extreme. The habit of over-independence feels good, and it's hard to give it up when Matt comes home. I never meant it to be hurtful to him, but it must have been. I'm sure it was another reason Matt felt he came home to an angry wife. For so long, I sucked it up. Crying and complaining wouldn't bring me anything but misery, and I found comfort in my newfound confidence and assumed power.

Sometimes I'm not sure we as spouses even know we are doing it. It is a survival mechanism built up over months of pushing down the fear that if something *were* to happen to our service member, we *would* have to do it alone. No room for, "I can't do it."

There is a balance in maintaining a couple's need for each other during a separation, instead of turning it off. Finding ways to continue to rely on each other makes reintegration much easier. On the other hand, as this soldier experienced, if we are too dependent, we never fully get to experience our own greatness. Finding the support we need at home doesn't mean we have to hide what is going on from our service member. It just means we take the emotions, problem solving, and details that would make them worried or powerless to someone who can actually help. Appropriate support can give us the ability to take our best to our spouse. Some of the support can continue even after our service member comes home, as long as we are openly communicating to our spouse to make sure the relationship is balancing out and reconnection is happening.

The scout and I continued to process and talk about how "need" in a relationship sometimes gets a bad rap. For some reason some people think it's unhealthy to need one's spouse, as if that makes a person incomplete or needy. The truth is, we all want to be needed, and our lives would be incomplete without each other. I thanked the soldier for the insightful conversation, his time, and his vulnerability.

After finishing the video, I determined my connection with Afghanistan was almost complete. I enjoyed a cup of coffee in the next room and resumed chatting with the scouts. I enjoyed their company, and our shared understanding of life experiences made it feel like home away from home. I feel the same when I meet a veteran or spouse. Few words are needed to understand what we have in common.

The soldiers in that circle were captivated by the irony that Matt and I had swapped places.

"You should call him!" one of them said.

"Call him?" I asked.

"Yeah!" they said. "You could not ask for a more perfect role reversal! How many times did he call you from Afghanistan and wake you up because it was the only time he could call?"

They were right. It would be 5:30 a.m. his time, and now Regina was excited about this idea as well. She took me over to a row of phones and said I could just dial the number.

I picked up the phone and thought how strange this was, calling my husband from Afghanistan. I was more than halfway through a busy day, and his hadn't even started.

The phone rang.

"Chaplain Weathers," he answered, which is what he says when he doesn't recognize the number.

"Hello, Chaplain Weathers, it's me." I smiled a smile he couldn't see. "Guess where I'm calling from?"

"Hey, Baby!" he replied sleepily. "Maryland?"

I smiled even bigger, thinking of how many times had I received similar calls from "Maryland."

"No, Fenty!"

"That's awesome . . . " he said, waking up only a little bit.

I thought about how much I expected him to jump out of bed at the sound of my voice and how he didn't. I was wide awake and excited about the symbolism of this phone call, but that didn't mean he would be. So many times I had tried to sound awake and excited when he called.

I could hear helicopters beating the air, circling Fenty, and I wished Matt could hear them. I knew how much that sound took him to his better memories of deployment. I wished he could stand here with me or joke with the scouts in the next room. I was emotionally raw from my connection with Afghanistan, but that didn't mean Matt would feel the same over the phone after being awakened from a dead sleep. I saw that some sacred spaces or gaps would never close. Just like I couldn't fully understand his time in Afghanistan, he could not understand my experience of Fenty right then. This was a shared place, but not a shared experience. I tried to explain to Matt why I was tearful over the phone, and for a moment I felt alone. We talked for a few minutes of the irony of our situation, and I felt someone peering in from the doorway behind me. Johnny was taking a picture of me on the phone talking to Matt.

"This is just too perfect of a moment," he whispered and then shut the door to give me privacy. I knew then: Johnny understood what all of this was about.

I took a couple of minutes to talk to our oldest son who was sleeping in our bed with Matt, because my dad was still there. It was great to hear his voice.

As I hung up the phone, I thought about some of my girlfriends who would very much understand my feelings of being in Afghanistan, and I knew I wasn't alone.

The members of the press and I packed up our belongings and headed over to the memorial where the secretary would emerge from his private meetings for a press conference. Two podiums and chairs had been set up on the left side of the memorial in front of the plaques on the stone walls. Afghan journalists were already lined up with their cameras ready to record the press conference. The American journalists I had been traveling with took their seats. Troops were beginning to gather around. This was a bigger deal than I expected. In contrast to the smaller more informal press gaggles on other days, this was a real press conference similar to those I'd seen on TV.

It seemed odd. From this end, it was just an event in this one remote place, but I realized it would soon be broadcast all over the world. The press conference would include Acting Afghan Defense Minister Mohammed Masoom Stanekzai. An interpreter would translate his remarks. One of the scouts motioned me over and gave me an extra earpiece so I could listen to Stanekzai's interpreter.

Secretary Carter began his remarks, thanking the Afghan minister for his coordinated efforts to train the Afghan army to do their part against Islamic State terrorism, preventing the spread into Afghanistan. The Taliban and Islamic State had been fighting, competing for territory in recent months. Stanekzai returned the thanks and read his speech into the cameras. He downplayed the overall threat of the terrorists but did say their propaganda could have an impact on the "morale of the people of Afghanistan."

Once again, I felt small in comparison to the world events happening around me. The policy I was watching unfold would directly affect the lives of the troops standing beside me.

August 20, 2009—Afghanistan

Today was an interesting day, it started early, as the Taliban attacked pretty much everybody and most of the polling places as a way to deter voters from getting out to participate in the elections. We responded in kind and let's just say there are probably hundreds of expired insurgents all over Afghanistan.

Things were calm around Bostick, though, except for two urgent local nationals that we had in the surgical tent today. Dr. Zagol has been in surgery for a good six hours today, and saved two lives. We had to do a call for B Pos blood across the FOB, and it was amazing how American soldiers responded so quickly. They didn't know that their blood was going to save some Afghan policeman they never met, but they came rushing in and definitely saved this guy's life. He had lost over 70 percent of the blood in his body. It was an amazing day, as I said, to sit on the sidelines and watch democracy being born.

I sat in the aid station and talked with the interpreter about his life thus far in Afghanistan and told him how honored we were to be a part of bringing freedom to his country, and you could tell he was grateful. Today made it all worth it.

Today people who went out to simply cast a vote for someone were shot at, mortared, and attacked. They were intimidated and scared, and yet went out to vote anyways. I won't ever take my vote for granted again, and I can see why veterans are so adamant about freedom and liberty and democracy. They have seen their friends die for it. They have watched men spill their blood for it. It is a humbling experience.

Hug those boys for me this morning, and please tell them that we are over here to make sure that mommies and daddies and little boys can grow up safe and sound, and free.

~Matthew

Before we headed over to the next event, I took a closer look at the plaques where the press conference was set up. I gasped when I realized there were *two* memorials for the 4th Infantry Division. The one I had posed with before was for another unit within the division. On the other side was another plaque dedicated specifically to the 4th Brigade Combat Team, *our* brigade, and a list of all those from our brigade who had been killed in action in 2009 and 2010. *This* is what Matt was telling me about.

I walked over and put my hand on the cool, smooth stone, overwhelmed by seeing all the names, many of them familiar to me. As I looked at the names, emotion gripped my gut and started to invade my heart. The lump in my throat returned with a vengeance. I ran my fingers over the names, feeling the carved letters: Fabrizi, Parten, Hardt, Kirk, Scusa, Martin, Mace, Griffin, Thomson, Wichmann. When I came to Justin Gallegos, I paused, remembering Amanda.

Amanda and I had stayed in touch since that horrible day. She had shown me grace, especially during that first year when I didn't have answers and she had every right to be angry. I did my best to listen, and the tragic moment we shared in her home bonded me to her in an indescribable way. Her courage and strength continue to inspire me.

Amanda eventually married again to another soldier, even after all she had been through. I continued to see her as the story of Keating evolved into a book, and two of our soldiers became Medal of Honor recipients. There are so many pieces, so many perspectives of the story that all come together in a magnificent tapestry of brotherhood and sisterhood. True community, giving all and then some, and overtaking that which seeks to destroy. Sitting in her home that day was my part of the story. It was the most vulnerable, fragile, sacred space that had developed for me. Amanda would forever have a place in my heart.

I recalled the small ivory plate Amanda gave me to mark the connection we would share for life. I thought of how it had shattered on the floor weeks earlier. Sitting with her in a moment where she felt shattered was a moment where my calling was confirmed. I would devote my life to stepping into the shattered moments of people's lives and helping pick up the pieces. It seemed only fitting that her plate, glued back together, scarred yet whole, was framed in a shadow box, hanging somewhere in my new home with a new purpose.

After the conference, we walked to the nearby hangar where the troops would hear from the secretary of defense. Helicopters continued to fly their distant circles around the base. We walked between the same looming cement walls I saw in Baghdad, except here they walled us in, creating closed-in alleyways to walk safely to and from the hangar and all over the base. I was back in the cement maze again. I walked up front with a soldier armed and in full armor. When I commented on the faint smell in the air that reminded me of incense, he gave me a strange look and sniffed the air.

"I don't smell anything," he said. "It must be just Fenty."

He had become inured to the smell. Nose blind. I looked at one of the journalists walking next to me.

"I smell it, too," he said. "I think it's burning trash."

"Probably so," said the soldier, "and waste."

I knew exactly what he was talking about. So much for incense.

At each stop on our journey, the host installation put on a showcase of its military power. At Incirlik, the Air Force had displayed various aircraft, including drones. Here, the Army had a UH-60 Black Hawk helicopter. At each stop, Secretary Carter spoke, troops had an opportunity to ask questions, and then many received a handshake and a coin from the secretary.

After the event at Fenty was over, it was time to leave. We were all surprised when we stepped out of the hangar into near darkness at 3:30 in the afternoon. Matt told me how quickly the sun set behind the mountains, but I did not realize it would be this dark. We could barely make out the C-130 in front of us, but we could follow the sound of its roaring engines. Soldiers with flashing orange lights on their chests indicated which direction we should walk. In a short three-minute walk to the plane it went from deep dusk to pitch black. We would have tripped on ourselves had it not been for the flashing orange lights guiding us.

"That was unexpected," said one of the journalists.

I smiled to myself. It was nice to know something they didn't.

On the flight back to Bagram, I made sure to sit by the window. It had been a long day and the dark sky made me sleepy thinking the day was over. I had lots to think about as we left Afghanistan. The plane rushed through the air just like the first flight in. When we got to Bagram, we still had a couple of hours on the E-4B to get back to Bahrain. I gazed out the scratched window and wondered how many troops had done the same on their way into a night mission, hoping it would be successful and they would get to come home. I thought about the scouts I met that day.

The pale yellow lights of Afghanistan below were surprising. I felt naive and bigoted somehow that I didn't expect the modern areas of Afghanistan to be so well lit. That was the downfall of having the nightly news as my only teacher, or relying only on pictures my soldier had sent. I thought about the turmoil beneath us in the cities below and wondered how many families prayed for the safety of their children.

As I stared into the night, a flare of light shot up from the ground.

That's not just fireworks, I thought. I didn't know what it was, but my imagination got the best of me. I was ready to leave Afghanistan.

No one, not even me, could have anticipated what it would mean to bring a military spouse, who has supported from a distance, so close to the front line. I felt as though I carried the weight of the spouses at home. I wanted to try to answer some of their questions.

We have all been affected by war. I didn't have anyone to blame for what had been introduced in our lives. It was life, war, and brokenness. But as the day progressed, I had also been reminded of what was given to us: friends forged through pain, a family to belong to, perspective on living, and a community to share our individual sacred spaces with. While there, I made my peace with my role as a military spouse. I made my peace with Afghanistan, too. As we flew over the mountains, this time in the darkness, I forgave them for what they had taken. I made a point to leave my resentment there the way Matt and so many others had left their innocence. I picked up something, too. I resolved to take back lost ground in my marriage, and to love with a new heart.

POWERFUL INFLUENCE

October 31, 2009—Afghanistan

I rode back to Bostick on the last seat in a Chinook with the tail down, full moon out, flying "nap of the earth." Sometimes the cool factor of the job is overwhelming. I feel bad for having a job that is this much fun. I will never settle for a cubicle again....

~Matthew

With a renewed spirit the next morning I felt lighter than ever, as though a load had lifted from my shoulders. I had made it through the day before in Afghanistan, and I felt my mission was almost complete. This day would be an exciting celebration, visiting two aircraft carriers out in the Persian Gulf.

The only access to the ships was by helicopter—another new experience, my first ride in a military helicopter. The press group was split into two manifests. The first group left around 5:00 a.m. I was grateful to be in the second group, which was leaving at 8:40 a.m. I had six solid hours' sleep, not enough to completely reset me but a God-given gift to me that morning.

At the airport, a Sikorsky MH-53 Pave Low and its crew in khaki flight suits checked us off the flight manifests. The first press group was already on the Charles de Gaulle, a French nuclear-powered aircraft carrier. I imagined them touring it in awe. As I checked in, I was asked to stand next to one of the lined-up chairs in the room. The door was open, and I could hear the chop of helicopter blades. I wondered if the crew was eager to walk us through our gear or annoyed at teaching us something they could do in their sleep. I wondered that sort of thing often throughout the journey, as I encountered troops who helped us acclimate to their environment. I opted to believe they were eager, because I was excited enough for all of us.

The crew walked us through the gear, seat belts, safety, and the importance of wearing goggles and helmets when we walked beneath the rotor blades. As I struggled slightly to put on my lifejacket, one of the secretary's security guards came over to help me. He was a stoic fellow; I hadn't seen a break in his cold countenance in six days. He didn't seem to mind that I needed help. He acted like a gentleman helping a lady on with her coat as he helped me put the strap around my body. I thought perhaps he was a dad to someone somewhere, and that he had to leave his family to be here, too. This journey opened my eyes to many civilians, not just troops, who left families behind to do jobs that also put their safety at risk. We were more alike than different. The journalists, contractors, and other civilians I met who served their country in various ways rarely received the attention, support, or credit that military families do.

We walked toward the MH-53 in a straight line like schoolchildren. The wash from the helicopter blades pushed against our bodies, although not as powerfully as the C-130 propellers the day before. I took my seat and immediately wished I could move to the back. The only two windows up front were on either side, just behind the pilots. The boarding ramp to the back of the helicopter pulled up but still left the back of the aircraft wide open, so the view from the back was the best. I took a few pictures, and others joined in. We passed phones around trying to capture each other sporting our goggles and helmets.

The crew chief, wearing a strap that connected him to the ceiling of the MH-53, remained standing up front behind the pilots. Another crew member was similarly placed and strapped at the back. The helmet tight on my ears dampened the roar of the helicopter slightly. The crew communicated via headsets from one end of the helicopter to the other. They smiled at each other and sometimes shook their heads. I imagined they were talking about how silly we all looked behaving like the tourists we were.

The helicopter rumbled and shook me side to side in my seat, swaying as it began to lift off. Before I was even ready, we were off the ground, rising straight up into the air so smoothly, almost like floating. I watched the crewmember across from me, sitting behind the pilot in a seat next to a window. I wondered if he still felt the excitement I was feeling during takeoff, or if that feeling had worn off over his years of service. Soon he got up to look out the window, and I watched his face. *I was wrong*, I thought. *He still loves it.*

I put my head back and closed my eyes, allowing my other senses to take over. I found I now looked forward to the diesel smell that accompanied our transportation to all these amazing places. The sound of the rotors blended with the smell of the diesel to form one memory. I've heard service members say that certain smells take them back to a particular emotional moment—for some, a moment of comfort and camaraderie, and for others, trauma. Our senses play a powerful role in creating and recalling memories. I was doing my best to imprint this one on my brain.

After a few minutes in the air, a few people took off their goggles. I looked to the crew for permission to do the same. Too loud to communicate verbally, they gave the thumbs up. I removed my goggles, straining to look out the back. From that view, it was apparent we were moving much faster than I realized. We passed over the whitewashed Mediterranean homes of Bahrain, and soon the white sands vanished into the blue waters of the Gulf. I couldn't tell how far above the surface we were. In the short ride to the aircraft carrier, I could not assess whether we were close to the water or if the waves were simply huge.

I wondered how the crew on board decided this was the job for them. If there was a "try this job on for size" day at military camp, I knew this would be it for me. Flying in a helicopter was not only fun, it was exhilarating. I understood why people signed up and went through months or years of training for this opportunity. I understood why service members look forward to the field or other "dress rehearsal" exercises, in spite of separations from family. This was an exciting job, and I kinda wanted to do it, too. I pictured myself in a tan flight suit, forgetting for a moment the ties that bind and fulfill me at home. It seemed this job wasn't on the front lines like the scouts I had met the day before.

I couldn't do that, I thought to myself.

Putting myself in harm's way didn't make sense to me. I love my country, *but I don't know if I love it enough to die for it,* I thought. *Might as well be honest with myself.* Then the next thought struck me, and I realized how shortsighted my thoughts had been; *helicopters like this often are on the front line, providing air support, transporting troops into battle, rescuing the injured, recovering the fallen.*

Rethinking my fantasy, I shifted the story line in my mind and pictured the crewmember across from me looking out the window for a different reason. This time there were seats full of Marines and special operators instead of our entourage. I put myself in the mind of an imaginary infantrymen strapped in the seat across from me. He was headed into an unpredictable mission, weapon in hand, helmet on head, eyes staring at the floor. He was ready to go, he had trained to go, and the adrenaline was pumping through his veins. I looked back at the crewmember near the window. Perhaps he would be doing the same on a mission, looking out the window, scanning the terrain for an unseen enemy.

Salt air flowed through the cabin as we flew. I felt a tug in my heart for the troops I imagined here with me. I thought of the families at home waiting for them. They didn't care about the excitement of taking off in a helicopter, they just wanted them home.

I want them to come home, too, and I would do it for them. I would go to the front line if it meant I could bring them home.

Returning to reality, I smiled slightly at the revelatory moment.

"I do it for the guy next to me," is the common response when civilians ask a service member why they are willing to risk their lives for a mission. They do it to make sure everyone comes home. Yes, they love their country. They believe in what it stands for, but deep down inside they just want everyone to come home. I sat up a little straighter in my seat, feeling like I had joined an inner circle of understanding. "I do it for the guy next to me," was transformed from a cliché to a solid answer, one I could get behind.

The helicopter hovered over the water, at least I thought it did, based on my limited view out the back. Then, we landed with a thud on something firm, obviously not water. We had touched down on the deck of the Charles de Gaulle.

The ramp on the MH-53 was smooth and, even in my hiking boots, I slid a little as I walked off the bird. A crewman grabbed my hand to keep me from busting my ass. I was especially thankful for that and the three other times it would happen that day.

My helmet and goggles were heavy and bulky, and I felt like I wore blinders. Even with a helmet, I wanted to cover my head as I walked beneath the blades, though they were a good five feet above me.

I took my eyes off the ground and saw the ocean. I wanted to stop and stare at the expanse in front of me. There was no land in sight, but I didn't have time to do a 360-degree check. Someone nudged me forward to move with the rest of the line. The bulkiness of the helmet made it hard to look down and see where I was putting my feet. The flight deck where we walked was crisscrossed with huge ropes, chains, and what looked like speed bumps.

When I finally could look up, I saw a row of French sailors standing at attention. I lifted my eyes higher and saw what looked like twenty more sailors lined up on deck and even more standing at attention on the bridge and the flag bridge. I'm sure we were quite a sight, as we stumbled onto their temporary home. The French public affairs officer greeted us with a handshake and welcomed us aboard in heavily accented English.

What a surprise and a gift to be aboard a French vessel during this week of visiting American troops. This ship was playing an historic role as the first non-American vessel to command a strike force against the Islamic State. Secretary Carter's visit highlighted the importance of the US partnership with France, especially in the wake of the terrorist attacks in Paris one month earlier.

As we walked down the narrow passageways inside the ship, we were greeted by sailors in blue uniforms with "MARINE" emblazoned in white on the back. They nodded to us as we passed by, stepping over the high bulkheads at each hatch or doorway. Moving down to the lower levels via steep ladders was no easy feat. We quickly learned, after causing some traffic jams, to keep to the right when going up or down to allow for two-way foot traffic.

We entered a small swanky room with wood wainscoting on the lower half of the walls and mirrors on the upper half. A bar and bar stools were in the center of the room, with plenty of seating at tables, booths, and chairs all around. This was one of four officer bars on board the ship. We were happily greeted by the rest of the press group who had spent much of their time here already enjoying steaming cups of French coffee. We were all surprised to learn that French sailors were allowed two tickets a day for alcoholic beverages on board the ship. American sailors don't have that perk.

More exciting to our group at that hour of the day was the coffee being served from shining silver espresso machines behind the bar. The French bartender, who spoke little English, must have thought coffee was a delicacy in America, given the way we swarmed around. For that week, it was a luxury of sorts. Our schedule gave us little control over what we might find to eat or drink. Finding a cup of coffee was a daily scavenger hunt. I joked with one of the journalists from the earlier group who always seemed to be the first to discover where coffee was being served.

An American public affairs officer I had not met before was joining our adventures for the day. She explained that the ship was nuclear-powered and capable of launching French and American aircraft. The vessel was conducting airstrikes in Syria and Iraq from its vantage point out in the Persian Gulf.

As I took my seat at the bar and waited for my coffee, a few French sailors came in and out of the bar area. They looked surprised to find their haven occupied by American civilians. One crewman was busy stocking the bar with Heineken. Another leaned against the bar in the corner. I asked if any of them spoke English. The bartender made a gesture to indicate "a little," but the one stocking beer shook his head. The bartender said something in French to the guy leaning against the bar. He came over and said he spoke some English. I told him about my project and explained that I would love to learn about what he does so that I could write about it from a military spouse's perspective.

As he shared his story, I learned he was a navy fighter pilot who flew one of the jets based on the Charles de Gaulle. His eyes reminded me of my brother, who followed my dad's footsteps to become a pilot.

Proud of the new perspective I'd gained of my father's job, I told the French pilot about my dad, and asked him to tell me more about what he does. He explained that he flew some of the nightly missions over Syria and Iraq.

I asked him about the experience of taking off from an aircraft carrier.

"There is nothing like it. It is my favorite part of the job," he said in a thick French accent, and his face lit up. He described the rush of being catapulted off the flight deck and the accomplishment of landing on the carrier after a completed mission. I'd heard the same from American troops: that part of the pull of a military mission is the thrill of loving the job, but another attraction is the satisfaction of a successful mission.

Admitting to being an army wife, I asked more about his work with the navy. He explained that each plane is loaded with a certain number of bombs to drop, based on the mission. Most times, he dropped what was expected and coordinated. Other times, though, a pilot was unable to drop the number loaded on the jet. The jet loaded with any bombs cannot land on the carrier.

"What do you do with them?" I asked.

"We have to drop them in the water," he said sheepishly, but then clarifying that this did not happen often.

As a clinician, I know there are often conflicting internal values at play in a mission that involves killing other people. I asked him, as sensitively as possible, how his love for his job is tempered by what he was asked to do.

He looked down, and part of the thrill of his job melted away.

"I obviously don't like that part of what I do," he said. "I don't like the fact that what I do hurts people. But it is what the mission calls for."

I hoped he had someone with whom to talk through those difficult feelings. I thanked him for his honesty and for his willingness to do a dangerous job to ensure the safety of both our countries and potentially many others. Hearing about this one pilot's role in the overall mission was powerful.

When I asked about his family, he said his wife was also in the French navy. They met in the service, and she was now at home with their two children. The French military also offers family programs to assist with childcare, health benefits, and additional resources for housing. He said his wife was very understanding of his job, mostly because she knew what it was like to be on ship. She had experienced deployment and seen his job up close. I appreciated having a glimpse into the similarities of American and French military lifestyles.

He said he felt fortunate to work alongside Americans within the task force. He was proud of the French military, but appreciated the experience that American service members have and was eager to learn from them. He had been to America for some of his training and was genuinely excited to be part of the historical significance of the French partnership with the US.

We laughed about how awful American coffee was compared to the cup of joy I was having right then. He recalled his first morning waking up in an American hotel.

"I was so jet lagged from the trip, but excited to go to school that morning," he said. "Then I brewed some coffee provided by the hotel and took a sip. I thought, *This is going to be a long trip.*"

Our time on the Charles de Gaulle was limited. We had just enough time for one of the sailors to show us around. He took us to the gift shop where we pooled our money to buy gifts for our family members. The prices were in Euros and I was thankful to be able to use a credit card. This was one time when it didn't matter how much a t-shirt cost, I was on a French ship in the middle of the Persian Gulf, taking something back for my boys.

From there, we walked to the hangar deck, below the flight deck, where many of the fighter jets were kept when not flying missions. I was amazed by the number of jets they were able to fit like puzzle pieces into a limited space. A walkway looking over the hangar doubled as an exercise area, including fitness equipment. There was an aircraft lift to move aircraft up to the flight deck.

When we were in the hangar, the elevator was up, leaving one side of the hangar open to the ocean with only a chain to prevent anyone from falling into the waters below. I had a brief thought that this was negligent. Anyone, especially children, could easily fall. Of course, I abruptly remembered, there are no children on an aircraft carrier. None.

I imagined what it would be like to grow so accustomed to this all-professional, all-adult environment and then return to home life, children, and civilians. Spouses can be baffled when a service member comes home and doesn't seem to notice that a door needs to be closed to protect a toddler. They may have forgotten household habits that are second nature to the spouse at home. How easy this would be to interpret this as the service member not caring, being disconnected, or insensitive. In reality, he or she has not thought about child safety for months. They need time to reorient to a new environment.

I wouldn't have this problem after being gone only one week, but I could imagine others feeling that way after months. Matt explained to me that service members deploy with the responsibility to maintain equipment worth millions of dollars and keep countless others alive, yet they come home and get fussed at because they can't load the dishwasher right.

We rode the elevator up to the top deck where our MH-53s were waiting for us. Two crew members I recognized from our flight out helped us prepare our gear. One mentioned he saw that I tried to see out while we were flying. He suggested that if I stood in the back of the line when boarding, I might be able to sit near the back. I was touched that he noticed.

Waiting at the back of the line gave me a few minutes to talk with both of them and thank them for the opportunity to experience what they do. They were both naval aircrew. I told them how incredible my day had been so far, but I wasn't sure they shared my excitement. When I asked what they wished family members understood, they mentioned that family members often simply don't understand what they do. I could see that. Standing on the flight deck of an aircraft carrier in the Persian Gulf, I agreed there is something families back home are missing out on. This was no ordinary day at the office.

All along my journey, I met service members like these crewmen who took special care of me. A protective spirit runs deep in the military world, and that's true for active duty members and their spouses at home. So many fellow soldiers have stepped in to protect or help me when my husband wasn't able to be there.

Matt Casper, one of our neighbors in Colorado, was the only soldier on the block who wasn't deployed. He became the neighborhood dad for so many families, hanging Christmas lights and taking care of minor repairs. Captain Steiner came to pick up me and my boys after I wrecked our car on the highway while Matt was deployed. He and his wife took us to their home, served us a warm meal, and then took my boys out into the snow for a snowball fight to help them forget the worries of the day. There are so many similar stories of service members stepping in to support each other's families while still maintaining healthy, appropriate boundaries.

I knew my husband appreciated knowing I was protected by professional military members during this trip. We talked about it before I left. He said it would be such an anomaly for troops to see a spouse there, and he predicted they would naturally be protective and interested in what I was trying to do. He was so right. I never felt unsafe during the trip, but I felt most safe when I was around the troops.

As the helicopter lifted off for our next flight to the USS Kearsarge, I watched as the two aircrewmen reached for their cellphones and took pictures of the view out the back. One later sent his photos to me to add to my blog and other writing about the trip. They allowed me to stand up and video the MH-53 flying the other half of our team behind us. Perhaps they enjoyed the moment, too, seeing it with fresh eyes. Like the French fighter pilot, the scouts in Afghanistan, and the maintainer on the C-17, they had important jobs. Jobs they loved. I hoped my enthusiasm reminded them why they chose their jobs in the first place. Strapped into my seat, I saw them let their guard down and enjoy the view again. At least that's what I liked to think.

On the brief flight over to the next ship, I thought about Matt. I love that he is a chaplain. I am so proud of him and how hard he works. He gives his all to those who are struggling to feel whole again, and I get to do it with him. I love that we are passionate about the same things and how our calling lines up with each other. I smiled to think of it.

I thought back on the number of times I received an email from him that sounded like he was not only in his element, but was doing what he felt created to do.

January 15, 2010—Afghanistan

... My duties as a chaplain are so rudimentary in comparison to the role I am allowed to play in their lives. I find I lead soldiers in worship just as much when we are talking about and enjoying God through the beauty of His creation in these austere mountains, as when we stand in chapel and sing his praises. When I awake in the middle of the night to bring them cookies and jokes before they roll out for a mission, I fulfill the task of being present, but I fulfill their hearts and remind them that God goes with them wherever they go. ...

~Matthew

So many times, Matt sat down with traumatized soldiers after near-death experiences, giving of himself. Even at home, he treats every person regardless of rank with the same attentive heart to serve. *How often had I told him that I felt that way about him and his work? When was the last time I saw his face light up while talking about his day because I was excited to hear about it? When was the last time I allowed myself to remember what it was like when we first felt the excitement of being in the Army and then helped him see the value of what he does with fresh eyes?*

Flying in the helicopter over the blue water, I decided that I wanted to renew the excitement of his calling, our calling—excitement that had been dulled by years of stress. Coming home, I knew I had the life-giving power with my attitude to increase his confidence.

TRANSFORMED

The ride was short to the USS Kearsarge, an American air-craft carrier within sight of the Charles de Gaulle that was also supporting the fight with airstrikes in Iraq and Syria. In spite of trying to sit near the back, I ended up in the middle of the helicopter. Oh well, I would have one more chance. I let the sound of the bird relax me. Our time on the Charles de Gaulle had been brief; it was only lunch time. Within fifteen minutes, we landed again with a thud. We were led off the MH-53 to a small door on the ship. Just inside was a ramp wide enough to drive a car down to the next deck.

Soldiers checked our names from the manifest to account for all of us, and we walked down the ramp toward the mess hall. I was thrilled to sit among the sailors and Marines for lunch and hopeful for at least one more opportunity to talk with another service member. The mess hall was small, about a third the size of an average elementary school cafeteria. As I walked away from the mess line, I was met with what seemed like hundreds of eyes all asking, "Who are you and why are you here?"

We split up with our trays, and I attempted to sit next to someone who looked friendly. Sailors in blue dungarees inter-mingled with intimidating, muscled-up Marines, reminding me of the first time I went to a military gym for a workout. Then and now, I tried to act like I knew what I was doing.

Groups seemed to gather in cliques by branch at the long rectangular tables. I sat down next to three sailors engrossed in their own conversation. Soon enough, the shortage of seats brought two Marines who put down their trays in front of me. One placed his Bible next to his tray and prayed, making the sign of the cross before his meal. I appreciated his discipline and his outward show of faith.

I tried to break the ice by introducing myself. The one with the Bible told me he was a military policeman. His job was to use a military working dog to detect explosives or illegal drugs. He was married and had a young son at home, only a toddler. The infantryman sitting next to him, with a mustache and dark hair, had a son as well and a daughter due to be born in the spring. He would miss her birth.

I congratulated him, while acknowledging the unfortunate news that he would miss the birth. Both men admitted they hated to miss the upcoming Christmas with their kids. The dog handler said his son was too young to understand why he wasn't home and asked about it on the phone every time they talked. He felt continuous guilt about his inability to explain deployment to a toddler.

The infantryman agreed it was difficult to explain to a child why Daddy couldn't be home for Christmas. He was obviously a tough Marine, but his family was one topic that softened him. Each man looked down at his hamburger in a way that reminded me of my talk with the pilots.

"You know," I started, "my two sons were two and five during our first deployment and my husband was gone for a year. Do you know that neither of them even remembers that year? They have a great relationship with their dad and always have, but the only memories they have of that year are from the pictures and videos I've shown them." I explained that even the second deployment while they were in elementary school has not scarred them.

Senior spouses have shared similar wisdom and reassurance with me in moments when I feared my kids were being ruined by our lifestyle. For a while I wondered if maybe these senior families just got lucky, that they had great kids who went on to function well in college. But I have seen most military kids adapt well to their lives.

Our lunch was brief as our sailor tour guide came to get us ready for the next stop on the itinerary. A tall beautiful female sailor with dark hair in a perfect bun offered to escort us to the restroom. I jumped at the chance and we began the long walk to the nearest restroom, which was on the other side of the ship.

We walked down the narrow passageways, shimmying past other Marines and sailors on the way. As an army wife, I wasn't used to the tight spaces these service members occupy on board. I felt privileged to see other service branches in action. I was excited about every detail, even down to the toilet. As the female sailor walked me up to the restroom, a male sailor stood guard at the restroom door.

"How did you get this assignment?" I joked, and he shrugged his shoulders as if he were still trying to figure it out.

On both ships, stepping over bulkheads and thresholds was nerve-racking. My hiking boots made me feel even clumsier. Life on board a ship is not for the claustrophobic, with so many tight spaces, low ceilings, and lots of close contact with thousands of fellow service members.

The female sailor and I headed toward the hangar where the secretary would speak to the troops. I told her I was a spouse and asked if she could give me any feedback on how her family was doing while she was at sea. She said she was from a very military-friendly family.

"Everyone has served," she said. "Everyone gets it."

Her dad was a retired Marine, her mother had served, even her brother. They understood why she loved it and why she had to go. She said they sent frequent packages and always seemed to know what to put in them.

She said her boyfriend, on the other hand, didn't quite understand why she would want to continue to do a job that took her so far away. The most difficult part was not being able to tell him where she was or what she was doing if it violated OPSEC.

"Today, for example," she said. "This is such an exciting thing for the secretary to come visit us, but I couldn't tell him. I can't tell him until it is over. Even then, I'm not sure if he would understand how cool it is."

She said he couldn't understand that when she is on the ship, she is always at work.

"It never ends." She said the sailors spend all day every day during a deployment working with and around their colleagues. "He wonders why or how I could be so busy, but I am."

Matt had said many times that he worked for a solid 365 days when he was deployed. I thought he meant he didn't get weekends or vacation time like people at home would. I thought he was taking a day or even two off when he needed it by going to his room and watching movies. I thought he was able to shut down for the evening at a decent hour.

Walking through the deployed experience this week, I could see that work doesn't end for deployed troops. Every day they are with their colleagues, in contact with those who have authority over them, and often called to duty at any hour of the day. No wonder Matt took off his cross patches on his flight home. He was exhausted. He needed to be off duty.

The sailor explained that it was rare to finish the work day at 5:00 p.m. and have the rest of the evening free to communicate with people back home. Even if they had time off, it didn't mean they'd be free at the same time the next day, or the next. I could understand service members asking a spouse for some grace in the expectations, some space in the schedule during reintegration.

After Secretary Carter thanked and greeted the troops on board, he conducted another press gaggle. A story was developing about some Iraqi troops who may have been wounded or killed on the ground during an American airstrike near the western city of Fallujah.

Immediately, I thought of the French pilot I met that day.

The defense secretary said it was an accident. He had called the Iraqi prime minister to express condolences, calling the incident "tragic."

He said, "I hope Iraqis will understand this is a reflection that things happen in combat, but also a reflection of how close we're working with the government of Prime Minister Abadi."

Early details seemed to indicate that the fog of war, as well as actual fog, were the causes of the incident. An official investigation was initiated.

After the gaggle, I reflected on the role of any of our troops who aim to do their job with excellence and yet are still human. Whoever carried out that mission the night before was now living in the midst of what would become their own sacred space. It would forever be a place where they would wrestle, perhaps a place their families could never go.

As we boarded the MH-53 one last time, I managed to get a seat closer to the back. I savored the remaining moments of this adventure. I paid attention to each of my senses, smelling the salt air, feeling the wind and the movement of the aircraft, seeing the waves below, and the other MH-53 flying behind us. The crew member in the back took a photograph of the USS Kearsarge for me as we left, a gorgeous postcard image of the huge vessel looking like a model ship in the blue water below the helicopter as we flew away.

My time aboard the Charles de Gaulle and the USS Kearsarge was the celebration I had hoped for. Of all the experiences I had hoped for on this journey, I didn't anticipate the bonus of seeing firsthand how the service branches work together. Seeing all of the branches of our military was an unexpected gift. This week allowed me to see our military from a big-picture perspective, beyond the playful rivalries, and how each branch depends on the other. I understood why Matt came home from deployment having made so many friends in other branches of the military.

Over the years, we've met people in passing who had helped out our Keating brothers. Regardless of where we go, we seem to run into someone who was part of the system that served 3-61CAV during that year. Those people immediately became family for what they did. Now I'd had an opportunity to spend a week in the company of outstanding service members who worked together for our national security. I was overwhelmed with pride for all of them and for the family members back home supporting them all.

We landed gently on the tarmac back in Bahrain, and I thanked the crew for an unforgettable day and for being willing to leave their families to accomplish their mission. We returned to the hotel in the afternoon, earlier than we had on any other day.

When I got to my room, I was eager to get in touch with Matt. The exciting day had been filled with the kinds of things he hoped I would experience. He had posted something on social media that showed how the role reversal was feeling for him.

December 16, 2015—Virginia/Matt's Facebook Post

First of all. I have no idea how she is doing it. Sure, there were sporadic moments during deployment when I hit exhaustion and still had to keep going, but each night as I watch the videos she uploads, she seems to still have so much energy. I would be dragging. Kind of like I am right now.

Corie would be the first to acknowledge that I sometimes work myself into a deficit. Okay ... most times. Some things that stood out to me over the past twenty-four hours:

Last night after taking the boys to see Star Wars, *we stopped off at IHOP. Corie messaged me through Facebook that she had just woken up and was available to chat for the next hour. Immediately, I felt a clock start. Either I excuse myself from the table and leave the boys to fend for themselves, or we rush through this late-night snack so that I could talk with her in the car on our hour-long drive home. I was trying to arrange the second option as the waiter suddenly became the most attentive server in the world. He just kept popping by with more questions. Is this guy interviewing me or something? Or does he just not get that I am trying to shut down this conversation, reserved for a later time, in order to feed these tired children who are now acting a bit drunk?*

I also became aware that I was surrounded by people. People whom I out-of-nowhere supposed were judging me for being on my phone and not prioritizing the feeding of my children. A few moments into that mantra, I gave that shame-train the deuces, and exclaimed in my head, "You can't judge me!" I immediately reflected and wondered, how often spouses of deployed soldiers have to attempt this crazy balancing act! It's insane, to try and be here and there?

Either way, it worked out, but still I was left to wonder: How hard it is to try and be the anchor for both kids, without being able to attend to your own stuff, or be replenished. Since we checked out of our own home like two weeks ago, to some degree I have been sleeping in the same room/bed with both or either of the boys (except for Air Force temporary lodging at Andrews ... that put the Army to shame ... sigh). Tonight, Aidan finally moves to his bed, and I will go to sleep early and sleep in. But I think about the children for whom their one parent is their anchor, and sleeping with or near them brings peace. And the parent, for obvious reasons, has a hard time breaking that habit, "I have to be there for them!" The constant awareness of others and their feelings becomes overwhelming. At least down range, you can clearly and concisely assert your need for quiet and isolation (though you may not get it). It is hard to help those little ones understand that Mommy/Daddy need a moment when they are not thinking about your every need ... all the while worrying about the safety/security of their own anchor who is far away.

I realize that it is not about the perfection of the house when she gets home (though it is VERY well put together, so far, I must say). I realize that it is about being healthy, rested, and ready to receive her when she stumbles off that plane.

I sent Matt a message to say I was available to talk. He was headed out to run errands, but was trying to find a place to stop. We used FaceTime so we could see each other, and I excitedly shared all the cool things I got to do. I felt myself wanting to hold back because I was having such a great time while he had been working so hard. I wondered if he had felt that way when he was gone.

He listened and tried to share some of the excitement with me. I could tell he was frustrated and tired. He had pushed himself so hard, and he was getting a cold. He was not going to be as well-rested as he hoped for my return. Matt hates getting sick, and he was frustrated at the thought of not being well when I got home.

I urged him to rest and take care of himself. I was excited to come home and help with the house, to care for him and the boys. I didn't care about whether the Christmas decorations were up or if the pictures were on the wall. He explained that he wanted to get as much done as possible so we could rest together. I felt helpless to ease his frustration. Preparing for and executing the trip had been "The Topic" for so long, and he was ready for it to be done and have me home. I didn't blame him. He had given me over to a project that was about us, but also took me away from him.

I remembered how I felt at the end of a separation and deployment. Exhaustion happens, especially when we got so close to the finish line. Nothing and no one was as important as getting our family back together.

Nothing I said now was going to convince him to slow down, because I knew what he was feeling. I decided to let him make the decision for himself. This would be the last chance I had to connect with him before the flight home the next day. We talked for almost two hours. It was a wonderful time of understanding each other and the first time we had a chance to process our thoughts together. As I told him what I had discovered, he just smiled and nodded his head like, "That's it. You got it."

Likewise, Matt's Facebook posts during my absence resonated with me and with other spouses at home who felt validated by some of his observations. We were in awe of the accidental strategy of our role reversal. We had not planned that from the outset. Certainly I would not have chosen the timing in the midst of a move, but it had been meaningful. The role reversal was brief, only one week, but powerful—and enough to begin a conversation. It was enough to appreciate each other a little more, enough to help us listen a little more intentionally when these topics came up again.

That evening, the press group planned to meet for dinner to thank Johnny Michael for all his work to set up the trip. All of the defense secretary's staff had done an excellent job executing every detail, a miracle of coordination and timing. I enjoyed spending time with them, knowing I had the rest of the evening to go back to my room for my final reporting. Sitting around the table with most of the press group, Johnny, and a few other staff members who showed up to hang out, gave me an opportunity to thank people for what they did well.

At the buffet, I encountered a Marine general who was also part of the group. He had been so focused on the job during the week, and I had been too intimidated to speak to him earlier. Seeing many senior military leaders in action overseas felt different from what I had seen in the States. At home, our senior leadership is very interested and engaged with military families. They care about how our families are managing. After all, they have families of their own. We see them address family programming and childcare issues, and always seem to make time to say hello or greet a spouse. They're so family friendly, I can easily forget that their mission is military defense.

Several times in the context of this week, I was in the presence of senior leadership and was in awe of the weight of the responsibility they carried and the focus they maintained. Senior leaders looked different in theater, in a good way. Here, they were in their element, leading troops. Like those they lead, they had to trust that what needed to be taken care of at home was being taken care of. They were not concerned with family programming, or whether childcare was available for an FRG event. This was a different environment altogether. Here the leaders were focused on the strategic mission in front of them. They were leading with a laser intent and the excellence that we entrust our service member's lives with.

Now that it was the end of the week, it seemed a more appropriate time to speak to the general. I thanked him for the amount of work he had put in to pull off an impressive week of traveling and scheduling.

He thanked me and asked me how my week was and whether I was able to see some of what I was hoping to see. I said it was more than I could have ever expected. I told him how surprising it was to see our troops genuinely filled with joy in what they do.

"I wasn't exactly expecting them to be miserable," I said, "but being deployed and away from their families with Christmas coming up, we make assumptions that they will be down. Back at home, we do everything we can to make deployment easier, and pity them for being far away. So, to see the spark of joy in the eyes of the people I met when they talked about their jobs was amazing. They didn't really need cheering up. They were happy."

His smile said I had figured out something he had always known.

"It's awesome, isn't it?" he said. "People have to remember that we are an all-volunteer force. Troops sign up to do it because they love it, or they wouldn't be here."

I thought I knew that, but I had never truly witnessed it.

Though I didn't say this to the general, I also realized while we were talking that perhaps no service member wants to tell his or her spouse at home they are enjoying an element of the deployment even when it takes them away.

Not too long ago, Matt and I admitted to each other that we actually look forward to some elements of our time apart, for training, field time, or even deployment. It was a strange thing to be honest about.

This was true some of my time at home during deployment. I enjoyed watching all the chick flicks I wanted, whenever I wanted. I enjoyed having the remote control. I enjoyed making decisions for the family—possibly too much. I enjoyed spending hours with my girlfriends. I still long for that. I enjoyed feeling a sense of accomplishment after a horrible day that I didn't think I would make it through. And to be completely honest, I enjoyed the simplicity of the long-distance communication between Matt and me that kept our conversations intentionally positive without the minor conflicts of everyday life. I've spoken with other spouses who admit the same things. After going through separations, I sometimes look forward to future separations, knowing I can do it when I have to. I've figured out ways to make it easier and ways to enjoy what I can and get through the rest. Even the most difficult moments, in hindsight, become the dearest memories.

Matt has admitted at various points that he longs for deployment again. I think that is why he gets that faraway look when he hears the thrum of a passing helicopter. I know he longs to test the skills he has honed in training. He and others long for the camaraderie that threads their hearts together during difficult times. They even long for the adrenaline rush of battle. As one scout told me, "It's like being in high school for a really long time, and then you finally get to come out and do the real thing."

Seeing the joy and spark in the troops I came across was the surprise that shouldn't have been a surprise. I knew that discovering purpose and calling was important for me and other military spouses. I had seen my own husband at a low point early in our marriage because he desperately needed to find and heed his calling.

This experience solidified the permission in my heart for

Matt to go when he is called to go. I will be okay when he focuses on the mission in front of him. I won't take it personally when some part of him longs for it. I know he would choose family every time if he had to, but I don't need to make it a win or lose or a choice he is forced to make.

The flight home could not have felt slower. I took an Ambien, hoping to sleep and reset my internal clock, which had finally consented to Bahraini time. I switched seats with the journalist who had the magical ability to sleep whenever she wanted, so I wouldn't be trapped in our row for the flight home. A clock on the wall showed Eastern Standard Time, and a countdown to our landing. Even though it was digital, I swore I could hear it ticking.

When I was awake, I made the rounds to thank the staff for taking a chance on me and for their hospitality during the week. I thanked Johnny for his idea to bring along a military spouse to see what I saw and report about it freely. Some of the staff commended me on my work, high-fiving me for the blogs they now had the leisure time to read. I was glad they were glad they brought me along.

After I finally fell asleep, one of the crew woke me up to invite me to the cockpit to watch an aerial refueling. I was happy to miss the sleep for that experience. One final time I marveled at the ability of our Air Force as two planes hitched on to the nose of our giant 747 to pump flammable jet fuel while flying 300 miles per hour. I sat still and quiet, as if just breathing would startle someone. I wanted the hands of the boom operators to remain steady.

Exactly as the countdown on the digital clock hit zero, our wheels touched the runway at Joint Base Andrews. Matt and the boys were within reach. They had watched the plane land. We were bused over to the passenger terminal.

Matt and the boys greeted me with "#TeamWeathers" t-shirts, Starbucks coffee, and handmade welcome-home posters, mimicking the end of a deployment. The journalists took photos and remarked to Matt how well I did during the trip. I couldn't have hugged my boys any tighter. There was so much to talk about. How would I begin? I was so exhausted; I was even too tired to cry.

On the two-hour drive back to our new home, I stayed awake by talking. We stopped for dinner. Without asking, Matt ordered for me so I wouldn't have to use any brain power even to think about what to eat. I so appreciated him knowing exactly what I needed.

When we got home, I took a shower and felt my body shutting down. I could have sworn I heard my brain tell me, "You have the count of ten to get into bed or I will shut this whole thing down right where you stand."

It was actually a very serious moment. I climbed into bed within that ten count and gave myself over sleep, feeling I had accomplished my mission.

The next morning, Matt had coffee and breakfast waiting for me. I was home, I was all his, and there was nothing to do but recover and walk our little family into the Christmas season that, for us, would only be four days. It was perfect.

With a wisdom that said he had been through this before, Matt gave me permission one more time, saying, "I want you to know I don't expect anything from you for the next three days."

I had a new perspective on what deployment meant for Matt and for our family. Some of it was the little things like seeing the cots, the DFAC, and walking on the gravel. Some of it was the thrill of walking in his shoes so I could know how exciting it was.

The longer I thought on all this, the more I understood the gradual steps of personal growth that Matt went through during deployment. Like the pictures he sent home that only gave me a frame of reference, I only had snapshots of how he was transformed over time. Was it possible I had also created inaccurate assumptions of what was going on inside him?

The day Matt called me at his lowest of lows, exhausted, claiming friendship with death, I thought he was falling apart. I wanted to buy a ticket and rescue him from Afghanistan. He was indeed at a breaking point, and it wouldn't be the last time. He was feeling his humanity in full force at that moment. He didn't ask to endure any of what he did, but that was what was handed to him.

From my perspective back at home, while I thought he was falling apart, he was actually at a crossroads. He had to decide whether to keep moving forward or do nothing at all. He could stay in the struggle or go forward and grow through it.

Matt certainly did skip through the posies with death. But first he had to decide what he believed about death. No service member goes in wanting to accept the harsh realities of war. Those in many career fields have to face evil, unfairness, and death in order to live out their calling. Military members, police officers, firefighters, EMTs, nurses, surgeons, the list goes on. Every one of them has to decide what they will believe, how they will handle it, and what they will do with what they see.

In those moments of wrestling through his faith, exhaustion, and shock, Matt chose to move forward and see what he was made of. At some point, he hoped the things that did not make sense would find purpose. I now understand that it was necessary for him to be transformed during deployment. He came home transformed—not broken.

As a chaplain, he *needed* to get to know this entity called death, its horrific ways, its movements and strategy. He *had* to become familiar with its silent and surprise attacks. He was joined in hand-to-hand combat and had to look into the eyes of an enemy that does not discriminate and is not fair. Ultimately, Matt was transformed into a *better* man, no longer afraid of death and its sting. As a chaplain, he needed to be able to hold death's hand, and by doing so he led the way for others through the valley.

What our unshared experiences did during this time kept me from seeing him emerge from that moment with a greater tenacity. I didn't get to see the joy of leading his soldiers through their own dealings with grief. I didn't get to see the spark in his eye and the smile accompanying a tear when a soldier left his office a little bit lighter. Matt was indeed different, and his transformation left scars that still ache and sometimes bleed. It came with a price, but it also refined his calling.

November 10, 2009—Afghanistan

I thought about today ... what an absolutely amazing existence I have experienced just today. Just in the last twenty-four hours, so many things that so many people won't ever, ever get the chance to do. Ride on a Chinook.

Pray with someone from another country. Laugh and joke with folks from two other countries. Pray over a little boy who passed. Attempt to resuscitate with CPR. Help out in surgery. Watch a live surgery. Watch a live video feed of bombing bad dudes. Eat a gyro with tzaziki sauce, and most of all ... be married to the most extraordinary, understanding, empathic, and strong woman a man could ever dream of, and to experience her love, compassion, and caring.

And THAT was the best and most exciting part of my day.

You have all of me, and as a result of this wild experience ... there is more of me to love in so many ways.

Go have a shopping spree, and buy something skimpy and pink.

~Matthew

The transformation that happened in me during this week surprised me the most. This was not just an opportunity to travel to see new things. It was an opportunity to open my heart, and I did. I made a choice to go, to want more for my relationship with my husband. I wanted to know what I did not know, and because of that my heart was softened. I left behind my entitlement and pursued him to the other side of the world just so I could understand him more.

What I found was that I didn't have to go that far. The simple fact that I wasn't content with the space between us was enough to draw us closer. Some gaps would never close, and that was completely fine with me now. But others could be closed, and they were more about what was going on in each of our hearts than what we had experienced when we were apart.

I was reminded that marriage is about constantly choosing and pursuing my spouse even when I am tired and think I can do no more. I can; I vowed to do it. I found there are still ways I can serve him, and we need each other more than ever. I allowed myself to be transformed by accepting the gift of hardship in our life that has given us the daily choice to be better.

Before, I thought there would never be a way for me to understand Matt's sacred spaces. By maneuvering around them, without realizing it, I had stopped trying to understand him. I found I could respect his sacred spaces even more by *not* avoiding them.

I came home with a better answer to his question, "Am I broken?" because the real question we bring to each other when we feel weak is, *Am I too broken for you?*

The question is actually, *Will you stay with me when things get tough? Will you be there when I can't do it on my own? Will you be the person in my life who will help me put the pieces back together?*

This is the power of marriage. I get to answer this for him, and he answers it for me. It is the most vulnerable place a person can be, and just the beginning of moving forward.

MOVING FORWARD

Just as Matt was changed when he returned home from deployment, I came home changed by my journey. It doesn't take a trip to the other side of the world to change a marriage, but it does take intentionality. I wanted to bring new life into what was already a good marriage. I wanted it to be great. I wanted to be changed by this project, and so I was.

If I wanted to understand my husband better and see his world through his eyes as best as I could, I had to be vulnerable as well as intentional. I had to set aside my own resentment over the ways Matt's deployments had changed him.

Before this trip, I thought I'd done everything I could to understand what Matt had been through as a military chaplain, as a man. I continued to support by listening and working around whatever I still didn't understand. But deep inside, my fatigue from our military experience made me comfortable with the gaps, as if they were unexpected guests in our home with a permanent seat at our table.

When two people marry, each is given access to the other's heart, but each must make a daily choice to open his or her heart to the other. To be that vulnerable is a risk, a risk of being misunderstood, taken advantage of, or hurt. Taking a vow to stay in "good times and bad, in sickness and in health" is simple, but when the hard times actually start rolling in, it is so easy to shut down and protect the heart rather than open up so we can better connect and support each other through painful times. No one on the planet can speak peace into a struggling soul better than a spouse. Instead of creating those moments of peace, many of us live with our hearts guarded.

We guard our hearts when we say:

"When he changes ..."

"When she stops ..."

"First, he has to show me ..."

"I can't until she ..."

Such preconditions keep us at arm's length from the hurts and each other. Marriage is one of the hardest undertakings we ever sign up to do. The calling of marriage is sacrificial, much like military service.

Undertaking this journey was my way of making the first move to close gaps in my relationship with Matt. I could have come up with plenty of reasons to show it was not my turn, but I chose instead to forget whose turn it might be.

I decided that letting love win was more important than my own victory. I resisted the temptation to see my spouse as the adversary instead of the battle buddy I vowed to serve alongside. Pursuing my spouse's heart is never a lost cause. I determined that the well-being of my husband was more important than my desire to protect myself.

When couples who care for each other appropriately are willing to risk vulnerability, the connection that follows has the power to heal almost any hurt. This is the power of marriage and an asset we take with us everywhere we go.

A strong marriage has the power to renew hope and build confidence as well as to speak deeply into the soul to affirm, "You are worthy of love." A faltering marriage has the power to crumble the reputations of military leaders, threaten our children's sense of security, distract our troops during deployment, and shatter the lives of both service members and spouses.

As a clinician, I sometimes see extremes. If a marriage is on a destructive path, the wisdom of professional guidance is often necessary to figure out the complex movements that need to happen. Anyone being mistreated or abused by a partner should seek out help and wisdom to figure out what kind of forward movement is appropriate.

Regardless of the extremes, however, healthy movements forward are always the first step. Every relationship has variables, and for each marriage the challenge is to consider what healthy forward movement looks like.

The biggest risk I took on this trip was opening my heart

to change. Fear of change was stronger for me than facing my initial fear of the giant C-17 or the trepidation I experienced during the aerial refueling. To see what I could do better, I chose to open my mind, knowing that what I learned would likely humble me. And that was scary.

Seeing ourselves as we are is naturally uncomfortable. Being willing to see ourselves as our spouses see us is even more so. Most of the time, there is truth in what we find when we see through someone else's eyes. Finding the courage to work on and change what we see is sometimes the best step toward making progress.

I could have continued to think of the gaps, the disconnect we were experiencing in our marriage, as "Matt's issue" and waited for him to do the work. Though some issues were the products of his job and his deployment, I held a significant spot in the equation. Denying that my own actions were contributing factors would have skewed the results and removed me from the blessing of healing and connection.

Marriages are not strengthened when individual spouses fight independently or avoid the fire altogether. The strongest couples are those who recognize they are fighting on the same side and agree to walk through the fire together.

The challenge for military families is that we sometimes walk through the greatest challenges of our lives while we are physically apart. When we're reunited, we play catch up, trying to get to know each other again and reestablish our relationship. Some of the issues we face are unexpected, and some we cannot prepare for. We're often unprepared for service members to come home with physical challenges or disabilities, as well as the hidden scars that haunt them. Spouses who become caregivers can grow quickly weary from the physical effort of daily service to a spouse, let alone the relational issues.

Whether there is injury or not, a couple can go through significant changes independently during a deployment. The longer the deployment, the more likely this is. Possibly, though, a couple's biggest transformation occurs during reintegration while trying to establish a new normal. We decide whether we will allow ourselves to settle into unhealthy patterns or establish new and healthy ones that take into account the ways we have each changed. As I watched from a distance, Matt was transformed by the crucible of deployment to the person he needed to be. I could choose to wrestle against it, insisting on what I wanted, or I could learn a new dance. And that is marriage for any of us. The daily ebb and flow of change and growth almost never happens simultaneously for a couple, even when they are not separated.

I grow, and Matt doesn't want to be left behind, so he grows. When I see him surge ahead, I make the decision to change. The hardest part of all of it is that we have no control over what the other decides. Ever. We influence our spouses, but we should never mistake that influence for control or try to use it as such.

Sometimes a lack of control causes resignation. Out of fear, we may choose to stay stagnant, waiting for the other person to make the first move. In this case, growth is impeded and bitterness develops.

When one spouse has chosen not to bring purpose out of his or her suffering, the other spouse may feel frustrated and powerless to create change in the marriage and move to an "I deserve ..." mentality filled with ultimatums. There is a time and place for absolutes, particularly in extreme or abusive situations. But for many faltering marriages, the feeling of powerlessness comes from a deeper place of hurt, from feeling misunderstood or discounted. Life should have been different. Marriage should have been different, filled with love and fulfillment.

My biggest fear is that when we find ourselves in that place, we will stop growing as individuals and instead breed resentment. Resentment is a powerful force that takes over a person and after a while chokes out available and accessible hope.

The challenge is the same for all of us: We can choose to move forward, toward our spouse's heart, rather than stay where it feels safe. We can be the first to make changes in our own hearts, to move closer to our own spouses rather than staying stagnant or cycling in old destructive patterns. By committing to our spouses for life, we promised to try.

Throughout life we have to choose to stay or go. Some service members who have been through traumatic experiences have chosen to stay in their pain, fearful of moving forward to get the help they need for healing. Is healing painful? Sometimes. Is there a price? You bet. Does it get better? Yes, it can, but it requires a choice to move forward and try. Hope shines most brightly in the darkness.

For the spouses of service members, the challenge is no less difficult. We have tirelessly held down the home front, making many sacrifices. Our marriages have been changed in many ways because of what our service members have been through. We've experienced constantly changing roles as our service members are pulled away randomly and for various lengths of time. Often, we protect ourselves by hardening our hearts, but then resentment settles in. We've read books on how to strengthen our marriages, how to be good military spouses. We've been to counseling to try to rescue our marriages. It sometimes feels like we are doing all the work.

Some may be tempted to hear *"If you aren't called to stay ... then go"* as permission to leave a marriage. When a service member refuses to get help, a spouse feels justified in giving up, wondering, *How much more can I take?* The very idea that someone would say there is more to be done only brings up more anger and fear.

A heavy rucksack of anger, resentment, and hurt might be laden with rocks labeled PTSD, grief, war, Afghanistan, Iraq, change, sacrifice, and many more. No matter who bestowed those burdens, the longer we hold on to them, the heavier they become. At some point, each of us has to decide we're ready to look into the rucksack to see what is in there so we can lighten the load.

To keep growing, even in a marriage that is already strong, both spouses must address gaps in their experiences before they become major conflicts.

A gap is what I call a space that separates a couple when there is misunderstanding. This can be something as small as not fully understanding a spouse's job or upbringing. Some are resolved simply by learning to ask the right questions. Others, as I've described in this book are "sacred," meaning they are based on traumatic or significant experiences that mark us or change us as individuals, for good or ill. A gap can happen any time for any reason and doesn't necessarily mean something tragic has happened. We experience various kinds of disconnects or gaps in marriage, some specific to military life.

For example, a feeling of separateness can develop when a couple has stopped listening to each other. Whether it is due to the busyness of life, a deployment, or something else, couples quickly find themselves passing like ships in the night rather than being attentive to each other.

The great news is that this is one of the easiest gaps to close. I can strengthen my relationship by choosing to be the first to try. This means listening as well as speaking.

Matt told me about a tribal custom in which warriors come home and sit in a circle to tell the stories of battle, while the rest of the village sits on the outside of the circle listening to the stories. The storyteller debriefs and is heard, and the listeners acknowledge that the battle happened. This is a beautiful picture of how a family can be supportive during reintegration or any other time the stories of battle are told.

Many service members who have post-traumatic stress find themselves back in a traumatic moment when they talk about the event and their senses come alive again. They can feel as if they are reliving the trauma. Interrupting to ask questions can sometimes be unproductive and increase anxiety. For complex trauma, I recommend inviting a professional into the conversation. A spouse can follow the village storytelling model by sitting in the room and observing what happens between the therapist and spouse.

On a smaller scale, everyday common misunderstandings can become giant minefields if they aren't addressed. Listen more intentionally or learn skills to speak thoughts and feelings more clearly. If the same topic keeps coming up in a relationship, chances are, someone doesn't feel heard.

Some gaps can also be mended through community. A significant event fuses a bond between people who experience it together. Military families are all too familiar with the bond that happens between battle buddies during deployment. As Matt and I experienced, many moments are forever etched in his mind, moments he spent with other soldiers who went through it with him. Regardless of how much he prepared for me to be his go-to person, I can never fully be his person for these sacred spaces. And that is perfectly okay.

The best kind of mending happens in the community in which a couple has bonded. Reunions, phone calls, emails, any kind of connections help to validate feelings and normal-ize thinking for both spouses in their separate experiences. These conversations and face-to-face reunions provide a place to continue processing what happened and to hold one anoth-er accountable to move forward in healthy ways. Gathering with those who shared a traumatic experience, and with their spouses, can provide a place to talk about anxiety and un-healthy coping as well as sharing successes.

I don't mean that a spouse who was not present for a trau-matic event is without influence. A spouse still has a powerful role, including the ability to truly listen and practice empathy. But a spouse may never completely understand and reclaim the gap. That's okay.

When I pictured Matt's moments on the C-17, putting my-self in his shoes, I felt empathy for him. Empathy can bring fresh perspective and new ideas for change. But I will never completely understand what those moments were like for him. They are not mine to understand, but I can listen and accept. Doc Zagol and others who were there with Matt will forever be part of the inner circle of his experience, as will many of the others from 3-61CAV family. My role is to leave room for those connections whenever possible so all of them are able to move forward healthily.

One of the most frustrating things that can happen in mar-riage is when someone needs help, but refuses. Regardless of whether it is due to something that happened in childhood, adulthood, or deployment, when it begins to interfere with rela-tionships and daily functioning, it is time to get help.

No magic formula exists that can make people ready to ac-cept the help they need. Everyone has a different level of re-sistance. For some, change will not begin until they reach the lowest point, where there is no other option. Every day, we hear about suicides among veterans and in military families. Some-times this happens when someone hits the lowest point and feels alone, unable to fight their way out. The role of loved ones is not to protect someone from experiencing the bottom, but to be there when they do.

Pretending everything is okay when a spouse is abusing alcohol, getting lost in endless video games, or any destructive behavior is known as *enabling*. Spouses enable when they hold back the consequences of a destructive behavior in a marriage or family. For example, spouses sometimes ask me what to do when their child asks why Daddy won't play with them. Rather than answer for the father, or worse, making something up, I suggest allowing the child to ask his father this question. This interchange may reveal to the father the reality that the child feels forgotten. Father and child can address the problem one-on-one, and the father will choose whether to re-engage with his child. Change may not be immediate. Building communication is a lifelong process.

The role of a spouse is to continue to support, but not enable or serve as a buffer, except when necessary to protect children. There are always consequences when a person chooses to not make changes a spouse asks for. Revealing these within the marriage can be powerful when done with kindness and love. Each should consider how he or she wants to be treated and try to do the same. Most of all, consider professional help to provide guidance to learn healthy boundaries.

Some gaps in our marriage are due to what we have been doing or not doing that may be destructive. We just haven't admitted it yet. I took this trip to walk in Matt's shoes, but my journey revealed more about myself than it did about my husband. The experience painfully revealed how many times I didn't really pay attention, the times I wanted him to change first, and much more.

Marriage is a mirror that reveals how our flaws and imperfections can impact the person we vowed to love. We have a choice to look in the mirror and accept what it shows us, or throw a blanket over it and call it a couch.

Denial is one pitfall. Shame is another. It's tempting, after the mirror shows us we are co-creators of disconnects in our marriage, to beat ourselves up, call ourselves names, or wallow in pity. Coming face to face with the things I wanted to change in myself has been excruciating at times, but the temptation to be swallowed into the pit of despair cannot be an option.

No one can rescue us from shame but ourselves. Expecting our spouses to do it is unfair. Brene Brown, a researcher on vulnerability and shame says, "Shame is the swampland of the soul." It has the ability to swallow us whole if we allow it.

The best thing to do is to own our mistakes, learn from them, ask for forgiveness, forgive, and move forward. Easier said than done, but it is a necessary part of moving forward.

Even if a service member does not have a difficult deployment and comes home with minimal issues during reintegration, life still has a way of bringing things into our world that invite us to stretch our character. Every experience is an opportunity to grow, no matter how big or small. Everything is grist for the mill. Make it count. We each have the choice to allow ourselves to be transformed for the better and then decide what good we can bring from it.

When Matt and I hold up our four fingers and say, "Fourth Quarter," I have lately been holding my hand up a little higher—not because we necessarily had the break or the rest we were hoping for, but because I realized that what we were waiting for was the end of the game. I've since decided I don't want the game to end. I want to keep playing. I'm on the field. All in and giving it everything I've got, for me, for my teammate, and my boys who are watching me play the game. Now when I hold up those four fingers, "Fourth Quarter" means I'm ready to play harder to win.

A SPIRITUAL REFLECTION ON THE POWER OF MARRIAGE

One of the mistakes I made early on in our marriage was to believe that if I did all the right things, I could avoid difficulty in life, especially in our marriage. A prideful thought, really, to believe I had any control over which obstacles we would encounter.

My mother-in-law's prophetic wisdom about what love is and how it matures over time definitely implied difficulty would happen. In fact, it seemed that difficulty itself would bring about opportunities for our love to grow. I didn't want to believe that. I thought if we made good decisions, we would somehow develop a fantastic marriage in the absence of suffering. I knew, according to what my mother-in-law said and the vows I promised, that life would present normal obstacles for us to endure together such as sickness or poverty. I also knew I had control over my own choices, whether or not to introduce dysfunction into my marriage. What I did not recognize then was the role pain and difficulty play in bringing a couple closer to the ideal God intends for marriage: a marriage that is sacrificial, life changing, intimate, and an expression of His love for us. It is in difficulty that we actually learn *how* to love each other. In this sweet spot, marriage becomes something powerful.

I love being a military spouse and all the joys of community it has brought into our lives. I was not prepared, however, for the difficulty that would come from extended separations from my husband and the impact of his witnessing the ugliness of war.

When the secretary of defense's office invited me to take this journey, I spent time reflecting on our military marriage. I generally thought we had done well with what life had handed us, especially by respecting each other's sacred spaces. But as I reflected on our own experiences of deployment, reintegration, and struggle, I felt more and more convicted to pursue a different answer for how to navigate the difficulty we, and other military couples, were absorbing.

The more I took a look at how we, at least I, handled what war brought to us, the more questions rose up within me. *Had I done all I could do? Wasn't there anything else we could do to feel whole again? We had learned how to respect each other, but could we love each other better? What was the source of this lingering resentment?* I realized I still had a lot more to process than I knew. I found that I had been operating out of a false belief that some of us, those impacted by deployment and trauma, were the unlucky ones. I felt we were given a "thorn" like the one Paul describes:

> *Therefore, in order to keep me from becoming conceited, I was given a thorn in my flesh, a messenger of Satan, to torment me. Three times I pleaded with the Lord to take it away from me. 2 Corinthians 12:7-8*

I figured this was something in our relationship that we would just have to endure. I failed to apply another truth, recorded by James:

> *Consider it pure joy, my brothers and sisters, whenever you face trials of many kinds. James 1:2*

I believe marriage is a powerful force when done well, and so I asked God to illuminate his design for marriage throughout this project, my journey. In essence, I asked him to show me the power of how marriage could be used as a vessel of change in a couple, individually and together. At the time, I forgot that those kinds of prayers are usually answered by God's invitation for me to be willing to change to find the answer.

My quest for answers during this journey was really a quest for understanding love. Loving is easy in the beginning, because it is self-centered. We fall in love mostly because we enjoy the feeling of *being* loved and finding acceptance from someone. As time goes on, particularly after marriage, we begin to see that our spouse is actually a mirror of our authentic selves, a mirror that most of us would rather not look into.

Our character, with all its flaws, is reflected back at us in the impact we have on our spouse. We see the hurt on his face when we say a mean word. We feel the emotional distance that is the consequence of our selfishness. There, in that reflection, we can discover that marriage is more about loving our partner than about being loved ourselves. It is also in this place that we discover we have a painful choice to make. I can refuse to adjust who I am and how I behave by continuing to be unloving, or I can sacrifice my selfishness and pursue my husband's heart.

In difficult times, we see more clearly on what foundation our values are secured. Values are the morals or beliefs we consider most important to us, the principles that dictate how we react to the world around us. We may say we believe firmly in the value of family, but when we are challenged to forgive a family member who has hurt us, that value may not be as unshakable as we thought. A devastating terminal diagnosis brings questions about life and death. A revealed extramarital affair brings questions about love and self-worth. The experience of trauma in combat brings questions about evil and the existence of God.

I can look back and see the many good choices Matt and I made. He talked to me about his sacred spaces and how they were impacting him. He let me know if his past was invading his present, so I could respond accordingly. I did my best to listen when he talked and to find ways to serve him in those moments.

When I am completely honest though, I know my internal reaction in these times was one of frustration. I didn't want to see him struggle. I didn't want this to be our life. I didn't want to have difficulty. I wanted things to be easier. This frustration, as I have learned, was rooted in resentment at the changes we were asked to make and how costly the war felt to me.

I had begun to feel that suffering wasn't worth it. This revealed my lack of trust in God, because he allowed this to happen in our lives. I needed to remember that God also had a plan to help us through the pain, ultimately to make us better for each other, but to also share that with others. I was not as secure as I thought in who I believed God to be.

In answer to my prayer for God to show me his powerful design in marriage, he exposed the cracks in my foundational view of marriage and took me on a journey to learn what real love looks like. When I thought about God's love for me, I kept thinking about how God pursues me with his love regardless of whether or not I am pursuing him or behaving well. He does this because he created me and says I am worthy of love and belonging. He is always there, always waiting for me to return to him. He is there to remind me that he already gave everything, even to the point of death to show me his love.

When I thought about what this meant in terms of loving and pursuing my husband that way, I was convicted. I didn't have the best track record with sacrificial love. I discovered I was much more selfish than I realized. Ephesians 5:25 compares Christ's sacrifice for the church to an act of love between a husband and wife. 1 Corinthians 13 speaks of love that is "not self-seeking." There are countless other verses that address the character traits of love, and selfishness is not one of them. If I truly believed that God's love is best revealed by his loving me so much that he gave his son, part of himself, so that I wouldn't die but instead have unspeakable joy with him for eternity, I couldn't continue in my own way.

I wanted Matt to know I cared deeply for his sacred spaces. I didn't want to see him fight this alone or collapse under the weight of it all. I wanted him to know I deeply cared about the state of his soul and how it had been affected. Was I willing to sacrifice my own comfort for him to feel loved on a completely different level? In order to do this, I needed to dig deeper into better understanding how God pursues and teaches us about love.

Throughout scripture and history it's clear God deeply honors commitments or covenants he makes with those he loves. He follows through with what he said he would do, even when those he loves don't hold up their end of the bargain. On my wedding day, I made a covenant with Matthew in front of God and witnesses to love and cherish what had been given to me. We didn't enter a static relationship in which we would merely live around each other without growth or work. We entered a dynamic agreement, a covenant that would be lived out by our daily actions. I honor my commitment to Matt by choosing to consciously move forward, bettering myself, drawing closer to God, and learning to love more intently. In turn, I also honor God.

God originally designed marriage to be a place of deep knowing and intimacy, safety and fulfillment. After God created man, he saw a need in him and said it would be good for him to have a helpmate and companion by his side (Genesis 2:18). God knew it was better for man to be in community. The gaps between Matt and me were keeping us from being in close communion with each other.

I started this journey to close the gaps I felt between us as a couple, caused by some of our separate experiences. I found during the trip that some of those gaps closed when I simply exercised more empathy with my husband's experiences. Although I had done some of this in the years following Matt's deployments, I looked back and realized that I may have grown weary and lazy. Military life, with its demands and transitions, was in full force, and we both found ourselves burned out. This burnout was a red flag that we were relying too heavily on our own strength rather than turning to God who knew better than we did what we needed. We needed to enter a season of resting and healing, but we were unaware of how to do that. The end result was that, in terms of loving each other, we were running on empty instead of drawing on God as a source of love and strength.

Leveraging my empathy the way I did while I was overseas was an extreme example of emotionally and mentally putting my husband before myself. I'm not implying that anyone should live like that all the time. In fact, it could be unhealthy for an individual to push aside his or her issues for too long. We are called to love our spouses, but we are definitely not called to worship them. Marriage requires a balance of sacrificial love and pursuing our spouse's heart, while also pursuing our relationship with God as Lord of our own lives. God's word clearly explains that from the outpouring of our relationship with Christ, we will learn how to love others better, especially our spouses. In his gospel, John recorded these words of Jesus:

"I am the vine; you are the branches. If you remain in me and I in you, you will bear much fruit; apart from me you can do nothing." John 15:5

The many emotions that welled up within me, especially in Afghanistan, surprised me. With the grief that surfaced for so many of the families that lost their soldiers, I found myself grieving over the difficulty and loss that many families experience when their soldier comes home. Some lose what they had before, the marriage they had before, and the outlook on life that existed before deployment. Military couples must go through a grieving process in these situations. We grieve for what we have lost. Matt and I managed our grief as best as we could, but the impact was strong, like ocean waves hitting a toddler. In the beginning, there wasn't much time for reflection and processing. That came only in hindsight.

My resentment, I discovered, was more about grieving the loss of what I wanted for us. Anger is a very strong step in the grieving process. After Matt's first deployment, there was a death in my heart that we would not have the easier life we had before—the life I wanted, the one I thought was better. And I had no one to blame. I couldn't blame the military, my husband, God, or even the people of Afghanistan. It was just something that happened.

After leaving my resentment in the mountains of Afghanistan, I discovered the ultimate source of my anger was sin—the fallen nature of our world—and its effects on my marriage. People choose destructive paths over loving one another. They choose war and power over the peace and salvation only God can provide. This isn't new. When the very first couple chose the destructive path of doubting God's authority and goodness, the result was death: death in their physical bodies, in their relationship with each other, and with God. They believed gaining knowledge and power would make them like God, but knowledge and power apart from God brought only destruction (Genesis 3).

In war, people hurt one another; they commit atrocities that are inhumane and purely evil. I had fully supported my husband joining the cause to serve those being mistreated, killed, and treated unjustly. But I had not anticipated the cost of what happens when someone is exposed to evil and death.

Death of any kind, but particularly violent death, is difficult to process. No one wants to witness a life ending too early. It is a reminder that we are all mortal and not promised life forever on this earth. Matt's experience of death gave him a new perspective on what it means to live each day to the fullest. Unfortunately, I didn't get to learn this with him, so when he came home, we had differing ways of living: mine in ignorant bliss and his in grateful knowing. As much as I wanted to get on the same page with him, I felt powerless to join his new outlook on life. It seemed I could never live fully enough.

This wasn't necessarily a negative change, but the conflict it caused seemed negative. I needed to grieve the loss of single-mindedness that only shared experiences can bring. I needed to grieve the fact that our relationship now included a source of friction that would make it harder for us to be united as one.

Recently, Matt and I took our boys into one of the caves of Virginia to tour the wonders of stalactites and stalagmites built up over thousands of years. We came across a pool of water so still that when we looked into it, it looked like an entry into another part of the cave. Then we realized it was actually the reflection of the ceiling. The water was only a few inches deep. Marriage is like that pool of water. Not because of its shallowness, but because of its reflective properties.

As I purposely sat in the pocket of Matt's deployment experiences, I also reflected back on conversations we had over the years. I remembered what he said about how he felt physically, emotionally, and spiritually during some of those times. As I did so, I found myself looking into that pool of water and seeing myself.

What I anticipated before I set out on my journey was a better understanding of my husband. What I actually discovered was the reflection of myself and how certain behaviors and beliefs of mine impacted him and our relationship. The previous resentment I experienced was not only a result of the loss I was grieving or my anger at sin in the world. It was also the sin in my own heart, my own selfishness.

Instead of finding ways to forgive in the midst of my grief and disappointment, I had allowed bitterness to take root in my heart. This bitterness leaked out through passive anger, resulting in withdrawal from my husband. By not paying more attention to the state of my own heart in this process, I was doing damage to our relationship. My reaction may not have been as loud as other expressions of anger, but it was every bit as destructive. I chose to believe I could direct my life on my own rather than trusting God for direction. I was focused on what I thought I needed from Matt and missing the true source of my resentment. When I didn't know how to understand his sacred spaces, when I just maneuvered around them, I was allowing those spaces to grow, pushing us further apart. I was also removing myself from the healing process God intended for me. At various points during the trip, I was able to look back and see how I could have handled situations better, how I could have loved him with more of a servant's heart.

In the revelation of a moment like this, I could go two directions. I could drown in shame: I'm a horrible wife. I should have done better. But shame was only going to leave me defeated and that is not what I set out to do. Honestly, it would have been a continuation of my selfishness, because shame is still about me.

The other direction is forgiveness, and it certainly seemed like a better option. I found out I had a lot of forgiving to do. I needed to forgive myself for not knowing how to handle the new complexity of our marriage, forgive myself for entertaining the resentment and bitterness that created the disconnect, forgive myself for choosing me instead of my love for Matt, and forgive myself for not doing things God's way. I would also have to ask Matt if he could forgive me for the bitterness I allowed to come between us. This was the beginning step of moving in God's direction.

I needed to forgive Matt for some of the actions that came out of his struggle to reintegrate from the "bizarro-world" of deployment. I had hoped for his perfection. I had hoped he could reenter our world unscathed and pick up where we left off, but he is not God. Only God can handle the complexity of good and evil and still be good, wise, and perfect, still loving and graceful. Matt was just as human as I was. In his own efforts to figure it all out, he had done amazingly well in some arenas and struggled in others. I needed to release him from the standard of perfection that I wanted and accept the messiness that comes with being in a human relationship. Neither of us will get it right every time, and I was seeing now more than ever that I needed to give Matt grace and accept grace from him. First I had to accept God's grace and live in the freedom from sin only his son could provide.

Jesus Christ came to Earth as a man to save us from the sin that is the root of all our pain. Christ experienced the peak of human suffering, and he understands the impact of every kind of evil we encounter: psychological, physical, emotional, and social. Even more, he experienced separation from God when he took on the weight of humanity's sins. He experienced our pain of feeling distant from God because of sin. Since he is also God, he is strong enough to defeat the sin that could destroy us. His death and sacrifice took away the fear that death would be the end for us, the finality of sin and separation. He gave us another way.

The resurrection of Jesus revealed that God's new covenant with us is fulfilled through his grace. Our only hope in this life is through the promises God has given us. Anything I hope for in life is futile if it is not in line with what God has already said. There are no new revelations of God. Only Jesus can provide the victory over sin we so desperately need in our lives. Only he has shown us how to love without being selfish, how to serve even our enemies, how to overcome the difficulty that life and sin present in our marriages.

To realize that all we can hope for is what we find in Jesus is freeing. For too long I had been trying to manage on my own strength instead of by God's grace. What I found by the end of this journey was that—in addition to being deeply in need of grace and forgiveness—I desperately need help to have the kind of love that can bring restoration and healing to my marriage. Doing it on my own left me exhausted, inadequate, and ultimately still revolving around myself. I needed a savior to save me from myself and show me a better way. I needed Jesus.

Before, I had hoped for the difficulties in my marriage to

just go away. Deep inside, perhaps I hoped that God would just resolve the pain Matt held in his heart. I think Matt would have liked that as well. I hoped that things would get easier over time. Although time can heal grief, loss, and trauma, some scars remain. Erasure isn't promised. Some of the things I was hoping for were not things God ever promised us.

When I set my eyes and my hope on Christ's fulfillment in my life instead of hoping for perfection in myself or Matt, I was free to finally embrace the difficulty that comes with living in a world that is invaded with sin: my sin, my husband's sin, other peoples' sin, and the consequences of all of it.

Jesus said, "In this world you will have trouble" (John 16:33). He never promised that following him would mean an easier life or a perfect marriage. Just the opposite. Marriage is a relationship that sometimes reveals our greatest weaknesses, reminding us we need his grace and forgiveness daily. The Apostle Paul suffered extensively at the hand of those who tried to destroy him. After asking God to remove the difficulty, or thorn, from his life, Paul writes:

> But he said to me, "My grace is sufficient for you, for my power is made perfect in weakness." Therefore I will boast all the more gladly about my weaknesses, so that Christ's power may rest on me. That is why, for Christ's sake, I delight in weaknesses, in insults, in hardships, in persecutions, in difficulties. For when I am weak, then I am strong.
> 2 Corinthians 12:9-10

So I find myself here: tired, weak, and seeing my true self in the mirror of my spouse. God invited me into a new kind of relationship within my marriage and also with him. He did indeed illuminate his design for marriage in my journey. His design was for me to learn to love like Christ and to see my need for him. In that, I could begin the power of true restoration that didn't necessarily mean healing. True healing and perfection will only happen when I am finally spending eternity with God in the absence of sin, death, and only the goodness of God. That, I can hope in.

But for now, I need to embrace the opportunity our present difficulty offers, an opportunity to extend grace, patience, forgiveness, and joy to my husband with the help of a loving and patient God. I am learning that I can extend grace much more easily to Matt when I allow him to struggle in his humanness. Grace is extending love and mercy instead of lording something over the other person. On Matt's worst days, will I continue to treat him with kindness the way I hope he will treat me on my worst days? Can I let go of the things I internally thought I *deserved* so we can wade through the mud and swamp of difficulty together? I will have to extend forgiveness more frequently in light of our shared humanness and sin, the way Jesus challenged his disciples to keep forgiving with no end.

I recognize the need for far more patience in this life than I can muster on my own. Growth in our character takes a lifetime. There are times when we are able to improve ourselves quickly, perhaps when we commit to eating healthy or exercising more. But there are other kinds of growth that take a lifetime. Overcoming trauma and our human reactions to the difficulties of life is an ongoing process. Some people may turn quickly to professional help, while others delay or avoid getting help at all. I am thankful Matt did not try to process our pain alone. As a clinician, I knew that moving through even the first deployment would be a long-term process. Yet, as a person deeply connected and impacted by it, I didn't want it to be that way.

God's timing is not my timing. Sure, there are times I believe God would want me to stop going in the wrong direction and do an instant about-face and go about it his way. But in his brilliant strategy, he knows the wisdom of timing. Matt's process of dealing with the deployment was not just about talking with me and a therapist about the traumatic things he saw. Although helpful, there is more to God's plan for restoration than that. Being restored doesn't always mean returning to an original state. Our history will always be part of our story. Restoration can also mean we are pulled back together, but with new character.

The camaraderie that comes with trauma is an integral part of restoration. The men who deployed alongside Matt are more than brothers to him now. The spouses who served with me on the home front are more than sisters. These relationships are priceless. Of course, we would love nothing more than to have those who lost their lives back with us. We cannot have that. The community and friendship we can have give meaning to the grief and pain that brought us to this point

Having no difficulty at all is not a realistic life goal. When James says we should consider it a "joy" to face trials, he also writes:

> (B)ecause you know that the testing of your faith produces perseverance. Let perseverance finish its work so that you may be mature and complete, not lacking anything.
> James 1:3-4

Trials and difficulty test our faith, what we truly believe. James said to consider it joy, meaning I can choose to see my trials as an opportunity for joy and purpose or get lost in the pain of life. I can now say that our difficulty has brought Matt and me as much joy as it has pain. It has brought friendships, growth, and the connection of wading through the messiness of military life together.

I started this journey knowing that Matt and I had sacred spaces in our marriage, and I wondered if having so many sacred spaces would eventually cause harm to our marriage. My sacred spaces and Matt's were set apart from the normal day-to-day experiences. They were significant moments when God had our attention. Whether it was because of the goodness of someone's service when we were in deep need or horrific encounters where we needed to believe there was still a good God, God made himself known to us.

The answer I found is that it's not the sacred spaces that could harm my marriage; it is what I do with them. The things Matt and I both learned about who we are and who God is in the midst of those sacred moments have been life-changing. Although some sacred spaces have the power to negatively impact our lives and marriage if we choose to let them consume us, they have even more life-changing power when we choose to draw closer to each other because of them.

Our sacred spaces will continue to call upon us to communicate more fully, love more selflessly, and grow more intentionally. This was God's design for marriage: that we would know each other vulnerably and intimately, that we would take on the call to be the vessel of his love for each other by following his example.

By the time I returned home from this journey, I realized we didn't need fewer sacred spaces, we needed more. I wanted to counterbalance the unshared moments we had been through, and those we would go through in the future, with a greater number of *shared* sacred spaces we would create together. If sacred spaces are significant moments where God moves through our lives to reveal himself to us, what better place for that to happen than in my marriage?

Yet it cannot begin if it does not begin with me.

"I have told you these things, so that in me you may have peace. In this world, you will have trouble. But take heart! I have overcome the world." John 16:33

ACKNOWLEDGMENTS

To the troopers and family members of 3-61CAV and the leadership of 4BCT, 4ID: Thank you. As time moves forward, my love and loyalty for you grows stronger. Our time with you holds some of our most sacred spaces, etched so deeply they have bonded us for life. I am a better person because of the grit, courage, leadership, and love we experienced with you. To our Gold Star families, thank you for letting me share your story. It is not easy to have your grief re-opened. May this project bring purpose out of pain. To Amanda Marr, thank you for trusting me with your sacred spaces. Your strength and resolve inspires me daily. I am blessed to know you.

To my publisher, Karen Pavlicin-Fragnito, and the team at Elva Resa Publishing, who read my first draft and saw the power of this story. You cast the vision, mentored me down the path of writing, and channeled my passion to encourage others.

To my lead editor, Terri Barnes: You have been Aaron to this Moses. God gifted me with you, breathing life into my words and lifting my arms when they were tired. You handled Matt's and my sacred spaces with tenderness and turned them into art. You and I shared a heart and a vision without needing to explain it to each other. Thank you for your patience, mentoring, and wisdom.

To Secretary of Defense Ashton Carter, Johnny Michael, and staff: I am eternally grateful that you considered the power of taking a spouse on a trip like this one. Thank you for caring about our families, for reaching out to me, supporting my efforts to share it creatively, and for believing that this could make a difference. Thank you for your own sacrifices to serve our families and country.

To Kate Dolack, Armed Forces Insurance, and Victory Media: Your support during my time as Military Spouse of the Year has opened opportunities I could not have dreamed on my own. Thank you for trusting me to represent you, for backing my strategy, and for investing in an opportunity that changed my life. You are paving the way for military spouses to live their calling, and I am living mine.

To my family and friends: Thank you for the incredible amount of support you have given Matt and me while we are serving military families. Thank you for stepping in to help us when we needed it and for your patience while we sought healing for ourselves.

To Matthew: Thank you for never quitting. For having the courage to stand with me and bring purpose out of suffering. For the continued grace when my imperfection shows. For teaching me how to love you and those around us. For delivering warm cups of coffee while I wrote furiously to tell this story about some of our most sacred moments, together and apart.

Finally, to our boys, Aidan and Jack: You are a beautiful reminder that no matter what changes around us, or who comes and goes in our lives, we are home when we're together. Your compassion, joy, and laughter always breathes new life into our days, and you have been patient as we grow up alongside you. We hope that when you one day read about these sacred spaces, you will reflect on our family with grace and understanding.